A Journey to Today

Finding freedom and discovering
the joy in the journey

DiAnna L. Gamecho

A Journey to Today

ISBN 978-0-578-91305-6

Printed in the United States of America

Published by
DiAnna L. Gamecho
406 6th Street
Pacific Grove, California 93950

T.A.S.K. 4 U & Me Foundation, Inc.
Together Achieving Successful Kindness
www.task4younme.com

I DEDICATE THIS BOOK...

To "My Princess", my pillar, my toughest critic, my best friend, my daughter, Rebecca!

To my son, Jacob, who always knows what to say even without using words! He is my anchor and my strength.

To my mom, Jessie, for never losing sight of my smile and always believing in what I do.

To my entire large family including grandchildren too, extended family, and those I call friends and honored to be in your life.

To all my mentors and teachers who encouraged me to "fail forward frequently" and stand up one more time!

To my project team, editor, Joyce Krieg, page designer and illustrator, Catherine Belardo, who helped make this book come alive!

A special thanks to all my "Cherubs" who have trusted every step we have taken together. You have changed my life as together we have changed a little piece of the world "one yummy project at a time".

And to the world of Rotary and my Rotary family -The Rotary Club of Monterey Pacific - for being a part of rescuing my spirit and changing my world. When I thought I would never discover that magical door of life, they opened not just one, but many doors that have guided me further in my JOURNEY TO TODAY!

I give to YOU ALL my greatest gift of gratitude!

TABLE OF CONTENTS

ACKNOWLEDGEMENTS

FINDING MY VALUES

I discovered my values with the guidance years ago from Stefan James of Project Life Mastery. I appreciate my values in the brighter light of today.

It started with a simple experience of answering a couple of questions as I was trying to gather and discover just what my values were and what they meant to me.

Stefan asks one simple question—what is most important to you in your life? He instructed us to write that one word, then think of another word, and the next and the next after that.

My very first word was HAPPINESS.

His next question was—why do you have the life you do? I instantly wrote, "Because I choose HAPPINESS.

He then said, "Now continue with the list of words. Each one is a value, what you feel, what you believe in. Those are your values. The first value on your list feeds the rest."

Then the words, my values, just flowed: Peace . . . joy . . . kindness . . . trust . . . belief . . . play . . . service . . . communication . . . honesty . . . vulnerability . . . gratitude . . . connection . . . passion . . . loyalty . . . faith . . . family . . . friendship . . . love and many more.

That lovely soul sure had some great points.

Values lead you to the life you have. Values are emotions that reveal what is important to us…

Values change the decisions in life.

Conflict promotes the values.

Stefan spoke of the hierarchy and how our values rank our priorities. What is your priority in life? Live your values!

He asked the following questions, which as a life coach I already knew to ask: "What do you want? What are you going to do to get it? When are you going to start?"

And I say: "Life is what you want. What is your vision? What are your values? Where did your journey start? Those are big questions!"

Every day when I walk out my front door for the day, I look in the mirror by the door and say, "Good morning, gorgeous, have a great day, beautiful. Love you so much!"

Call it silly as you may, yet that is the nice way I start my day! How can you not start a happy day when someone has already said good morning, calls you gorgeous and beautiful? What better person to do that than YOU?

Stefan told us we should always have a morning ritual. Funny he would say that, when I already knew my morning ritual. A million websites are out there to guide and speak to you. Just research "happy morning rituals." You will be amazed at what is out there. Even better, you can courageously discover your own ritual to see what makes you smile first thing each morning.

In conclusion, I know that lesson with Stefan opened the door of truly seeing my values in a different light. Now that I think about it, that lesson in listing to my values, along with this book, is my reward, acknowledgment and confirmation that I have discovered, applied and embraced all of my values.

This is how I have gotten to this point in my life — This IS my Journey To Today!

INTRODUCTION

YOU are a gift to this world! Your name is a gift that brings the meaning of YOU to the world.

A few of my gifts are: delightful, daring, deliciously delirious, darling, and divine. That is just a bit of me. "D" is for DiAnna and it has taken my entire journey to discover all those yummy words that describe me.

Who are you? I invite you to think of your name and find all your gifts that start with your same initial. Example: "D" for delightful. For you, Sierra, "S" for scrumptious. For you, Bekki, "B" for beautiful, bold, bright and brilliant. Whatever your name, have fun discovering the "Y"—Yummy YOU!

I hope this journey to my today gives you a sense of the sensational you, and that you are able to relate and reveal the steps to your today.

I challenge you to stop before you read any further. Get a piece of durable paper to make a bookmark, right now. Put your name on it and follow with all your "yummy" descriptive words.

Your name is your virtue. It is your birthright. It is who you are to the core. It is your road map to your journey. You get to start discovering the real you simply by having fun for a few moments of play.

If you do not know the story of your name, who named you, why they gave you that name, and what your name means, enjoy discovering that and then give yourself permission to step into all of the GREAT YOU! Own it, live it, LOVE IT!

Then keep that bookmark in this book as you turn each page of my journey. You will not lose the page that marks a similar situation in your life. Give yourself permission to let go, let loose and let love lead your way to discovering the joyous journey to your today.

I applaud every one of you for joining me on this journey and acknowledge your courage to face any adversities along the way as you discover and become awake to the journey you have been on all your life.

ADVERSITIES, VALUES & VICTORIES

Love leads it all.
Values change the decisions.

What are your values? Why do you have the life you do? What is most important to you?

Where do you want to go? What are you going to do about it? When are you going to start?

Those are all questions I have asked of myself. As I discovered my values in life, I discovered my peace, my joy, my love, my passion and my purpose. I invite you to join me on my JOURNEY TO TODAY.

Each chapter is a SHORT STORY and features a specific value and a song. As you read my story, you will realize they have never guided me wrong.

The way I see it and have always been told, when you want to make it real, you have to own it! You have to name it, you have to put sound to it. For me, I put music to it! Whatever the experience, it makes it more profound!

❝

I have a dream that my four little children will one day live in a nation where they will not be judged by the color of their skin, but by the content of their character.

❞

Martin Luther King Jr.

CHAPTER 1

A CHILD IS WHITE, A CHILD IS BLACK

Value: Communication

I believe communication is the key to all success in all relationships, in all parts of our life.

"You can read me like a book" that is what I have always said. I wear my emotions on my sleeve! Yep, call me naive or better yet "gullible Gamecho" because I trust, I believe, and I always give everyone the benefit of the doubt until they give me a reason not to, then my mind says "what's next?"

Being strong in my beliefs yet as flexible as a puppet on a stick, you can pretty much guide me, convince me and tell me what is next if I feel it is good to my soul.

When I was a child I watched the movie PINOCCHIO… It actually scared me. Being from the south I learned you always tell the truth, you always show respect, and you always read your bible verses.

That movie made me think as a young child, if I did not tell the truth my nose was going to grow and I would get in a lot of trouble. So believe me, I made sure I always told the truth. I thought for sure with my nose being the center of my face and feeling it was a large Italian nose, it was going to define me for the rest of my life so I better be good and always tell the truth.

My poor nose. It has had its share of adjustments. No, not for Pinocchio's reason.

The first time was when I was boxing with boys and guess who got a broken nose? Yep the only girl with boxing gloves on. The stubborn little redhead who would not "go down" when hit. I was not going to let a boy win. Did I say I was the only girl in my family? My brothers were going to teach me "how to be tough."

A cast on my face, no Junior Prom and six weeks later I was a little tougher. That was my first bout thinking I was tough!

Then as an adult the big "C" came to fight! Yep, cancer in the center of my face! Skin cancer on my freckled nose. A nose I felt I took care of because I didn't want it to grow like Pinocchio. Was the cancer getting back at me because I always complained about my big Italian nose? I felt my nose was too big for my face and now I was faced with questioning myself "am I really that vain?" "What will I do if they have to take half my nose" my mind went wild.

"does the wood maker really have the magic it will take to make my world better than my mind can define?

18

The day came they thought they could take it with one "margin", cancer talk, and they actually had to do five "margins" to get it all. YES, there was a big hole in the center of my face and then they said "we cannot close the hole, the plastic surgeon must come in"... WHAT!??

They "patched" me up and sent me over to a man that was the perfect "wood maker" as in Pinocchio. He was able to put my nose back together. He said "we will do a half face lift using the skin from your own face and you will be good as gold", "WHAT? ARE YOU KIDDING ME?" He was not kidding!

Going into surgery the next day all I could think of was "what will my face look like after the surgery"?

Not knowing if they really got all the cancer out, not knowing if the "wood maker" could really put my nose back together and trying with all my heart not to feel vain! I was a mess!

They kept saying "if you have to have cancer, this is the best one" My thought was "Yeah, right in the center of my face"! My mind went to a different place.

It is funny especially when you are under the influence of laughing gas where your mind goes... I knew it was not going to be laughing gas I would be under, it would be general anesthesia for a surgery.

I also knew it would take me to a place in my mind that would make me think "does the wood maker really have the magic it will take to make my world better than my mind can define."

That night I felt like I swirled into the whale's mouth like Pinocchio, dreaming of life's past and hoping for that magical future.

I was spinning with thoughts and seeing my life flash before me.

When I first flashed back, it took me to my younger years. It opened my eyes to a journey that has led me to today.

Being born and living in Mississippi as a young child had its own challenges. At times I lived in the fight or flight mode. I really could not remember too much of my challenged little life. At age five we moved to Florida, I felt pain inside and could not figure out why.

I would ask myself "why don't I know what this feeling is?" "Why am I always scared?" Where is my mom and my brothers?" Questions I did not get answers to, till many years later.

The south had its own challenges with separating people. Not children from their parents yet different colors of people. I recall being upset because I could not play with a little "dark girl."

I knew in my little world that white people were not allowed to speak with "dark people." I never understood that! I liked everyone and did not see a difference in people. Even at an early age I saw many colors in my "rainbow and unicorn world" which kept me safe, kept me protected from scared feelings and it kept me in a place I could be happy without hurting.

At the early age of seven, my mom told me we were leaving Florida. I remember her saying "You and I are going on a vacation, the boys are staying here"

Of course I didn't ask any questions because you never question your elders when you live in the South. And besides, who wouldn't want to go on a vacation with your mom and no boys".

Back then I did not really understand after two weeks of "visiting" my uncle, why my mom left and left me there?!?!?

Before she left, she said "I am going to the boys, I will send for you in two weeks" Again without questioning I said "okay."

I did not see my mom and my brothers for well over a year later.

After she left I then received my "wings" from the airline pilot three times as I flew from Wisconsin to California to Illinois then finally back to California. I went from one member of the family to another in that time frame which felt like an eternity.

Little did I know my grandma' would not let my mom have me back till she got through her demands in life. It was not till my older years I discovered after many years of feeling abandoned that actually my mom protected me from a life that was not fair to little ones or her. She went through a challenging time and my grandma' kept me away from all that.

I sure did miss my mom and brothers. I was scared of my past so I really did not miss much more than them.

This all sounds bad yet I was in a good place, protected and in a joyful world with Uncle John and his family. Not ever knowing him or my auntie, they quickly became my surrogate parents in the absence of my mom and for that, I am blessed and forever grateful.

At that time in my life, I was a very tiny freckle faced, curly redhead with a southern accent that kept you entertained. I became very spoiled or as I would rather say, very loved!

At the age of nine I flew with my grandma from Wisconsin to California to live with my Aunt Geraldine who then registered me for school. I remember so clearly walking to school as a very scared tiny white girl with a bright yellow dress on. I recall arriving at school and hearing about a very important "dark person" being shot to death. Everyone was crying and saying lots of things I did not understand. I sure was scared they might shoot me.

All I knew this day was how scared I was, feeling very alone and asking myself the same two questions "are they going to shoot me?" And "where is my mom and brothers?" This was a terrible day in the world, when we lost Martin Luther King, Jr.

My mom did return from Florida with my brothers. She found her strength and back to Illinois with Uncle John and Auntie Jeannie.

I acquired many air-miles by the time I was ten! I was now on my way from California back to my mom in Illinois. I was so excited and could not wait to see her.

Once again we were all one BIG happy communal family. At least in my world we were all happy!

Back then I could not understand why did my mom always have to work night shifts? Why was she always tired? Why did she always seem sad?

Did I mention my mom is one of 13 siblings!

On the road again my mom, brothers and I were on our way back to California. Now going to Uncle Allen and Aunt Ruth, more family I did not know.

Again being the respectful little southern girl, I never asked her why and she never spoke of it...none of it! Instead MANY YEARS went by as I watched her work many hours to keep us four kids feed, housed and whatever extra she was able to provide, she did! If she couldn't "someone" in the family or friend, or sometimes even a "Fairy Godmother" always made sure we did not go without. Life was tough and I would consider us poor yet we really were very rich with family and so much love amongst us.

After several years of communal living, at one point in a two bedroom, one bath house with seven kids and three adults. Let me tell you, IT WORKED! There was so much love in that home. Aunt Ruth kept this little land of pure love in check. We all knew what we were and were not allowed to do. That included NEVER calling food "garbage" if we did, we got a second serving and was not allowed to leave the table till we were done.

This was also a time in my life when music became my world. It was my way of communication. I would hide the pain in music, I would find my joy in music and I would dance till I was exhausted. It was something I would do to release crazy energy I didn't know what to do with or even understood what it was all about.

My biggest regret was forcing my southern accent to go away!

I still had a very strong southern accent in the 5th grade and I was bullied in the California school for "speaking funny." My character was certainly challenged. I would say "hey y'all" and they would laugh, tease me and even pushed me around because of how I talked. I would go home on many occasions crying.

It was the gift of Uncle Allen and Aunt Ruth that changed my tears of pain to tears of joy.

I would come home many days from school and would find Aunt Ruth and Uncle Allen having their own little "sock hop" and all the neighborhood kids would join in. My aunt and uncle served up awesome Rock n' roll lessons as my brothers, my cousins, the neighbors and I, all learned through dance, music, and lots of discussions around the dinner table, what was important in life.

Years passed and I found my "true love". Or I thought I did! Was it love or was it a way out of a town that I could walk out my front door and get sex, drugs or rock n' roll, not my uncle Allen's kind of rock n' roll.

We were all known as the "Madison Avenue Brats" it wasn't a bad place, just sometimes bad things happened. However Uncle Allen made himself known to the big drug dealer down the street as he made a personal visit to Danny's front door telling him "I have seven kids in that house right down the road, if anything happens to any one of them, I know where you live."

Guess who became Uncle Allen's good friend? Really!?! No one ever messed with any of us kids and Danny really was a nice guy.

During my years in communal living and facing all the challenges and JOYS, the one thing my two aunts, aunt Ruth and auntie Jeannie did was always made time for talking and listening. Not that I shared everything because there was so much I could feel, yet could not remember. And even though my aunts gave me that safe place to talk, it was my mom who I needed to communicate with.

That was not happening and it is that, that was causing so much pain in my young adult life. How can I find the answers to so many questions if she didn't talk!?!

I always felt I did something wrong or I did not do enough to "earn my place" in the family and for a very long time felt she gave me away. What else would a little six year old feel who was not told what was really happening?

COMMUNICATION IS THE KEY to all relationships. Good, bad or indifferent (age appropriate). Always communicate!

We will not always like what we hear.

I believe, do not ask the question until you are ready to hear the answer. Even if you don't like the answer, it is then that the healing begins.

"Only the Strong Survive"
Jerry Butler

66

The best way to find yourself is to lose yourself in the service of others.

99

Mahatma Gandhi

CHAPTER 2

I WANT TO SERVICE

Value: Service

Is it possible, can you really do it? Can you imagine confronting your gremlins and telling them, "Be gone!" How simple would that be?

My gremlins almost got the best of me when I was in high school. We had that infamous Career Day that most high schools have. I remember the instructor in front of the room asking everyone, "What do you want to do when you grow up?" At that point, I really had not given it much thought. When he got to me, the words just came out. "I WANT TO BE A MOMMY!" He laughed out loud and said to the entire class, "DiAnna wants to be a mommy, so she'd better marry that doctor in the back row."

I was so humiliated and embarrassed, thinking "being a mommy" was not enough!

Now that I have confronted my gremlin of NOT BEING ENOUGH, DOING ENOUGH, OR EVEN KNOWING ENOUGH, I have accepted I am just who I am and happy being the momma I am!

Lo and behold I am a mommy of my two beautiful and successful biological children, one foster child, one youth exchange daughter from Spain, two exchange daughters from China, three Nicaraguan daughters, and 600 plus students every year at school.

I work in the office of a high school and feel I get paid for being "mommy" whenever needed, which is every day for one reason or another. The need for a simple Band-Aid, a kind word saying, "It will be okay." and, yes, even sometimes, a lot of times, a big hug. Besides managing my office and keeping track of all those cherubs in attendance, I am a "professional mommy." What is that doctor who was in the back row doing today?

Sad to say, school is not what it used to be. In some areas, it is so much better. In others, not so much! There was a time when the teachers were right and were able to speak their minds. If a parent was rude, the teacher could "give it back to them." Now the students and parents have so much to say and more! Sometimes they will say things just to get their way and parents .... Well, they are always right, right! WRONG!!!! Yet in my office, I truly try to make every wrong right in my little Southern style.

In all my years serving in the school district, I really have had only three hard-to-handle parents who actually made me concerned about my safety and well-being, and I did indeed "get 'em with kindness ...." They didn't know how to receive that kindness. I definitely caught more flies with honey those days!

One time I even wore a tiara so the parents could see me in a crowd while troubleshooting registration. A very tall and angry woman approached me, but she could not stay mad. She was looking down at me. Did I mention I am 4'8" TALL with shoes on? She tried so hard to be mad and to yell, yet faced with a woman wearing a tiara with pink stones and a big smile saying, "I understand and I will do what I can to help you," she had to turn her face and smile.

Who can be mad at a smiling freckle-face wearing a tiara?

Who can be mad at a smiling Freckle-Face wearing a tiara?

Over time, still having so many emotions in me that I was trying desperately to identify, I just kept taking that step each day to discover the emotions. Sometimes I was more scared than I wanted to admit to. Scared of what, I didn't have a clue. Moving forward to discover what emotions…I didn't have a clue.

Until one day I woke up out of a sound sleep and said the words out loud, "I WANT TO SERVICE."

My husband looked at me and said, "What? You want to serve, you want to be a waitress?"

I quickly responded, "No, I don't want to be a waitress. I don't know what that means, I just want to service." I lay back down and went to sleep.

After that awakening, I could not get it out of my mind, and my mind kept spinning. What is service? What does that mean? What does it mean to me?

I must admit, I thought service was about police officers, hospital employees, even teachers who share life skills. At one point I thought you had to get a paycheck to confirm you were "servicing" someone. Maybe that is why my answer to that question, "What, you want to be a waitress?" was "NO." At that point, I did not know what "that service" was. I didn't know what it meant to me.

I found myself really paying attention to that question. What is the definition of service? Webster's Dictionary (remember those hardback books where we would get lost in words?), believe it or not, has 21 definitions of "service." I will give you one: "Service: A useful result or product of labor that is not a tangible commodity."

What is my definition of service? It is simple:

(S)erve above self

(E)ngage in areas where very few will

(R)eceive the love you give

(V)ictor over those who do not accept the word "no"

(I)gnite with light

(C)are when no one else does

(E)xpect nothing in return

Not knowing what it meant when I said "I want to service," I just kept giving of myself.

Reflecting back, thinking I was not servicing, I realized I was actually servicing with each hat I wore:

Endless service of love as a mommy.

Service of loyalty and commitment as a wife.

Joyful service at my desk as Ms. G.

Cheerful service as Coach Gamecho.

Authentic service as auntie.

And fun service as a friend.

I certainly woke up to the fact that I "service" in all I do because in each area I give all of myself! Certainly not because I expect anything in return. I give all of me, as I know I have given all of me to the need!

That is what I believe service is.

Do I always feel like I am enough in my service now? Oh, heavens no! It is an ongoing process, yet I am more awake to it when that emotion comes to play. Have I given enough of me?

Fortunately, I am surrounded by so many beautiful hearts and souls who see my heart, who are as sensitive as I am, who stand beside me and guides me and loves me for who I am, and that is enough in the service I do. And when it is not—I stand up and say "Tada— what more can I do?"

Being you in service is ALWAYS ENOUGH.

John McCain, the late U.S. Senator from Arizona, put it so profoundly: *"Nothing brings you greater happiness in life than to serve a cause greater than yourself. Tie yourself to a cause that's bigger than you. You'll have adventures and satisfaction and joy in your life."*

I know for me when I "service" it is a great joy in life!

"Love, Serve & Remember"
John Astin – Remembrance Album

"

*The journey of a thousand miles
begins with a single step.*

"

Lao Tzu

CHAPTER 3

A TASTE OF HEAVEN

Value: Courage

Picture this: standing in my kitchen enjoying the crazy loud chaos of cooking dinner surrounded by lots of family. Two biological teens along with four extra teens who needed a home, all running around chatting and requesting my attention. As it is all going on, I felt something inside. I heard a voice and it was not one of the six kiddos.

I felt "something" come over me. Something inside, not butterflies in my tummy or pain in some part of my body. It was as if something "or someone" was screaming joyful words "Go, just go."

I stopped in my steps and tried to listen. To what, I had no clue at that moment. Less than two minutes later, my mom came into the room and announced out loud, "I have some free airline miles. If you could go anywhere, where would you go?"

Oh my word! Without even taking a breath, I shouted out, "MISSISSIPPI!" Everyone stopped and looked at me as if to say, "Are you crazy?" Especially my mom!

Who goes back to a war zone if you don't have to?

I thought for sure at that moment, my mom would walk out of the room. Instead she said "Okay…" Then my daughter and my two nephews all said, "I want to go".

What? Was it really going to happen? Is this one of those "be careful what you ask for" moments?

Whatever it was, I was going!

Why did I want to go to Mississippi, you ask? The answer is quite simple, yet extremely complicated. The last time I saw my dad, I think I was six years old. Now at 41, I couldn't even imagine what it would be like to see him.

Four months of planning, saving money, making travel arrangements and a lot of praying followed. I remember asking God every day if this was the right thing to do. Am I opening a door that should stay closed? Would I be accepted and wanted when I arrived? What would I do when I got there? But never once did I ask God why I had been called to go. I was very open-minded and open-hearted with no expectations. I was fragile yet very strong. I knew I had to find my courage to take the next steps.

Four months seemed like an eternity! I was patient yet on a rollercoaster of emotions. Each day, knowing that the good Lord was beside me, leading me on this journey, I knew in my heart He would not leave me.

As the time got closer I began daily to ask God to send me an army of angels. An angel for travel, an angel for strength, an angel for support, an angel for joy, an angel of sight and awareness, an angel of guidance and an angel of love.

I knew I was asking for a lot and hoped that He would answer all my prayers.

The journey began on a cold, rainy night on a flight out of San Francisco. Frightened and tired, I sat in the airport with one of my most precious gifts from God, my daughter! My mom and two nephews sat across from us, talking. I was focused on my next step.

It was dark and cold and I did not want to get on that airplane, yet I knew in order to get to my destination, this was the path.

For a split second I thought, "I am out of here. I am not getting on that airplane." Then I remembered my prayer, asking God for an angel of travel. I then knew it would all be okay.

We flew through the night, changed airplanes and slept on uncomfortable airport chairs, meeting nice strangers, seeing more of the world other than just our little town. I became more excited as the morning drew near. I could hardly breath thinking of what was about to happen.

Finally we were in Mississippi! Wouldn't you know it, I instantly felt the angel of guidance. I knew it the moment I stepped into the terminal and saw two very special familiar people, R.J. and Aunt Doris. I knew my journey was starting off wonderfully!

They looked at me with the most warm and welcoming smiles and said in their beautiful Southern accents that I loved, "Hey Sissy."

I knew I had entered heaven. I felt I must have died on that airplane and God was letting me see peace on earth before leaving. The very sound of the name "Sissy" echoed in a place in my heart I thought I had lost forever. Still taking one step at a time, I heard God say, "Don't worry, I am here beside you".

The first day in D'Iberville I found myself saying to an angel, "Pinch me, I think I am in heaven" and the angel replied, "No you are in the Hot Tamale Stand." I not only felt the presence of my most precious Nana (my dad's mother) and her continued tradition of making and selling the best known tamales in Mississippi, but I also was awakened to my childhood. Before I knew it, I reconnected with my beautiful little Southern inner child.

"Sissy" reappeared!

Pinch me,
I think
I am
in heaven

God sent me two angels. One was my most precious cousin R.J. When we were children we were hooked at the hip. I remembered when, I'm guessing maybe age four or so, we entertained the family by dancing to American Bandstand. The other was my Aunt Doris, as beautiful now as she was back then as she just smiled so angelically, looking at R.J. and me together again.

The level of love at that moment was overwhelming. These two angels on earth took me to the place of enlightenment, and a place of my roots. Santini Street! A home of my past. What memories.

R.J. and I strolled to the buoy as we had done many times before and this time it was with great joy and excitement. My eyes were wide open and my heart overwhelmed with joy that we were together again as we were as children.

They always say God sends you angels as you need them! Boy, was He gathering them quickly!

As we were on the streets of Biloxi, another smiling angel walked up to us, Philip Cornelius, known to all as "P.C." He welcomed me with the most wonderful smile, saying, "Yes, I know where your dad is!" My heart stopped! Was I ready for this? This is what I traveled so many miles for.

When the night came to a close, another angel arrived back in my life. This angel was another cousin, Felicia, whom I did not know long as a child, yet she made me feel so loved. She truly wanted to be a part of this special journey—me reuniting with my dad.

The second day of this journey, I said to my angel, "Pinch me, I think I am in heaven," and the angel said, "No, you are in the presence of your blissfulness, the tremendous love God intended and planned for you." Little did I know on this day I would have yet one more instance of welcoming love. I met my angel of joy! Shanna, R.J.'s youngest sister, was not born yet when I left Mississippi. She was joyful and wanted to be a part of what we all felt way back when. She sure brightened the lives of everyone around her and warmed my heart with that bright light, a light of continuous hope.

To add to that blissful feeling, that afternoon I met one of my half-brothers for the first time. Amazingly, he looked so much like my own son. He had the warmth and charm-filled smile that opened yet another part of my heart. He was not only very welcoming and eager to share in the excitement of meeting up with my dad, but he said the words I never thought I would hear from him "You are the sister I've always wanted!" My heart melted. I knew I had to be in heaven!

Later that night I met a quiet angel, another cousin, Michael, who came in quietly and left quietly, leaving behind a warm sense of love and happiness. Could you believe it, the family kept coming in. All with smiles, warm hearts, bright eyes and curious.

As that evening came to a close, I thought: "How could so much love and joy be gifted to someone here on earth?"

The third day was gracefully quiet yet filled with peaceful joy. This day was blessed with the giving of gifts. One red rose, a garden angel statue, a book of wonderful words, and an Easter bonnet of love. Giving material gifts is a fun thing to do; receiving the gift of love is incomparable!

Sharing in all the family homes, walking through peaceful properties, seeing magnolia trees and the quaint little river running through the yard, the tree house and baby chickens. Walking with the wild rabbits and seeing the deer tracks. It was all so peaceful and fun.

Later that evening the crawfish were biting and the candy apples were calling at the Crawfish Festival.

Spending quality time with so many angels has to be a sign
of heaven!

Closing my eyes that night I prayed: "Dear Lord, please let him
want me, please let him love me. I forgive him, Lord, for all my pain
and sorrow. I ask you, will he know who I am? Will he want to see
me? Do I really want to do this?

This is what I came for, am I ready? Oh dear Lord, please don't
leave me. Please be beside me. Please give me the words to say to
him. Thank you, Lord, for being in my heart and never leaving me.
Amen!" With that, I closed my eyes for the night.

The morning came. This was the day I had waited years for. I was
without words. I didn't know what to say or feel. I wasn't afraid,
yet every muscle in my body was tingling. When will he get here?
What will he look like? Will he recognize me? Will he want to stay?
Since this was to be a surprise, so many thoughts where swarming
in my head.

I kept smiling as everyone started arriving. The family had arranged
a barbecue so he would not think anything was out of the norm.
It was a slow start, yet all so wonderful. All my angels must have
gotten on the phone and called every family member you could
imagine. I could not believe all the people who came to see me and
my bundles of joy from California: my beautiful daughter, my two
nephews, and my mom.

The warm hugs, the great smiles, the support for the reunion was
more than I could ever imagine. I still didn't know how it would

happen. I only hoped it would happen soon.

I turned and there he was! My dad! A man I only remembered being afraid of. A man who was bigger than life, then. The energy in the room was beyond all the energy on earth. The love and support in the kitchen was more than any earthling could ever dream of.

Then I heard one of my angels say, "Uncle Dave, there's your daughter!"

He asked, "Where?"

The voice said, "There."

I was standing right in front of him. He looked at me and after several questions and eye-to-eye contact, he knew it was me as soon as I said, "Hey there, it's me, Sissy."

The world stopped!

He'd had a stroke not long before this meeting and I was afraid he would have a heart attack. Instead, he embraced me and the world started revolving again. I thought I was going to have a heart attack as my heart was beating so fast. Together again after so many years … Thank you, Jesus!

The day was incredible. Besides the great chef, there were many questions, many conversations and lots of hugs and laughter. Aunt Rosie told stories and we enjoyed great banana pudding! How could life be so wonderful? How could someone feel so much love in one day? How could someone who caused such pain and sorrow now generate so much love and happiness? This must be the work of God and His angels!

This day was all too short. He had been out of my life for so long and now back in it. The hugs I felt and the words I heard, "Isn't she so beautiful" and "I love you" was more than a dream come true.

At the close of the night, I recalled for a brief moment the release of the fear and the overwhelming blanket of love and support. It was breathtaking. Not only did I get my dad back into my life, I also heard the voice of a mother I never knew. This couldn't be earth; I knew I had to be in heaven.

A time for forgiveness and reconnection

I have always been a "talker," hardly at a loss for words, yet this night and every night since the beginning of this journey, all I could say to the Lord at the end of the day was, "Thank you, thank you so much, thank you!" My heart was filled with joy. This day, being Palm Sunday, I was given back a part of my heart that only God could make happen. This will be the most memorable Palm Sunday ever.

Now that this special journey was more than half over, my heart became sad. I didn't want to leave or even think about leaving! The next day began with tears.

With the joy of getting a father back, came the sadness of a mother. Not understanding and not taking on my mother's "stuff" for the first time with my angel of courage beside me, I stood tall! Now I knew the purpose of this journey. It was to enable me to let go, to forgive, to grow, and to move on in life. I had to accept the hugs of a father and the hard words from my mother.

At the end of a beautiful day that I believe she enjoyed, I believe she was also hurting. She let me know that by saying, "How dare you accept that man who hurt us all."

I knew she was hurting and I did not want to add to that pain by fighting with her, yet I did get very defensive. I yelled back, saying in the best way I knew how that I needed to take these steps to fill the void in my soul, even if it hurts. She released more feeling, which I believe helped her heal a bit more.

Seeing all the pieces of the puzzle come together this day, I totally understood and appreciated her view, yet I needed to move forward.

With two days left and time to play, that's just what we did. The Easter bunny's smile and the shopping mall made for joyful pictures and was enough to distract anyone from a place of sadness. Red beans and rice hit the spot and a quiet warm evening on the porch swing with a bright shiny moon was a sign that this was a special place in heaven. How could I leave a place filled with so much love and the roots of my soul?

Now it was the evening before the last day of my phenomenal journey. The day was long and filled with questions. Will I ever come back? Does he want me in his life? Am I worthy of love? Will I ever be the same? I turned and said to my angel, "Pinch me, I think I am in heaven."

The angel replied, "No, you are in a place of comfort, pure contentment and happiness. God planned this for you, so enjoy it now without questions."

Red chicken stew, old pictures, lots of laughter and a time for memories were the greatest gift of the day. Times were tough and the separation was long, yet the love that grew within me never skipped a beat as I sat there with two fun-loving angels, R.J. and Tina. The children sat in the background listening to stories of times past, wondering if it was all true. What was true, was the love that was felt at that table, the heart that was filled with joy, and the grace that only God could have given.

The last day began with big smiles as I didn't want it to end.

The tamale stand was open and running as I sat as my Nana did and rolled my first tamale. The laughter was loud and the sun was shining.

A bike ride would only add to the gentle ease into a new outlook on life. A smiling angel, R.J., rode in front of me, guiding me with powerful words yet listening with an open heart.

After sharing a special place under a willow tree, and giving me a clipping that would go home with me, the time came to say goodbye. Standing there in complete awe I turned to my angel and said, "Pinch me, I think I am in heaven," and the angel reached over and whispered, "No you are not in heaven; however, God has given you a taste of heaven right here in Mississippi."

This was an unbelievable journey as I discovered how Sissy, my inner child, resurfaced with joy, busted out of a bubble and learned how important it is to take one courageous step at a time, even when it hurts.

I think I will take inspiration from the words of G.K. Chesterton: "Angels fly because they take themselves lightly." Do we really want to travel this journey of life with the weight of the world on our shoulders? I know I cannot fly to my future of fun unless I take myself lightly. This is when I tell myself, "Enjoy the ride with your hands up and fly, babe, fly!"

"I Hope You Dance"
Lee Ann Womack

"

*You can't be real unless
you accept reality.*

"

Denis Antonio Ruiz Menza

CHAPTER 4

GUILTY AS CHARGED

Value: Belief

For years I remember having the same two dreams. In one, I was a little girl on a swing attached to the clouds. I would swing really high, then I would fall off the swing. I never saw myself hit the ground. I would just fall and wake up with a terrible feeling. In the other dream, I would see myself as a tiny little girl resting on an ocean shell in a glass bubble, not being able to get out. I would pound on the glass and no such luck. I could not figure out how to get out, so I would lie back down.

I never did figure out what either one of those dreams meant, and it really does not matter at this point.

However, as I was studying my Life Coach course, I learned more things about myself than I would have never imagined. I thought I was going into training to learn how to coach others. Silly me, what was I thinking?

Through many years of hearing, "You live in a fantasy world," and truly protecting myself in my "rainbow and unicorn world," a lot of times I did hide in my safe place. My place was colorful, bright, and joyful, and a place where I laughed a lot. My unicorn always allowed me to rest on his back and he would carry me when I was so tired with emotions. The colors in my life kept me bright in my time of darkness.

Every time I would hear those words, "You live in a fantasy world," I would take offense as it would darken my "rainbow world." In a time of despair, I would think of Thumper in the movie Bambi. "If you don't have anything nice to say, then don't say anything at all." My "Thumper Theory" kept me focused.

I really did not understand those words till I went through my Life Coach training. I was doing a class exercise where I was instructed to bring my stuff to the table. I had to be the client.

Oh, heavens no! Our instructor was so wonderful at what she did. It was no wonder she was in front of that room training us! The activity called for us to role-play being both the client and the coach. I was the "client" first. I tried to pretend to be someone I was not. There was no way I was going to bring my stuff to the table. There was no way I was going to show these class members who I was and the pain I had been holding for so long. Especially when I could not identify most of the pain I was feeling.

Little did I know, with a simple exercise (at least, they said it was simple) to draw my utopia home, how it would open my eyes! She said to draw a house with five floors, each floor being better than the previous and the top floor being your ultimate dream floor. She said, "Don't hold back." With my colored pencils, I began to draw.

The instructor was leading us all the way and telling those role-playing as the coach the questions to ask us as we drew. Oh, my words, there was no pretending at that point. It all started coming out in colors to include the dark room. As we completed this exercise, I kept hearing her say, "This is your fantasy world, this is your utopia, this is your real world and the world you get to choose to live in and be all of who you are."

When she said that, I sat there and realized, I am guilty as charged! I am living in a fantasy world and it is my real world where I choose to be happy, no matter what is going on.

I am not going to allow the darkness around me to take over the colors in my world.

I am not saying all the color and happiness is fake or not truly coming out in a genuine way, because it does. I am saying I am not going to allow the darkness around me to take over the colors in my world.

My world is not always bright and it is not always filled with jolly joy, yet I am able to step back, stop and look at my world as it is in that moment, asses what I believe is happening and know that it is okay if it is not so bright today. I know living in a fantasy world is sometimes looked at as a little "crazy," yet I believe the crazy ones are the ones NOT allowing themselves to live in that place of joy.

I have been asked several times in my life, "Do you ever get mad?" I actually had to think about that before I could give it a genuine answer. My answer was, "No, I do not get mad; I get hurt."

They have also asked me, "Do you laugh all the time?" My answer is, "Yes, I try to every day."

Sometimes I believe I am "too much" for some people because they really do not understand where I come from. They don't get my ability to see so much good in all the bad.

I remember early one morning my husband, at the time, who had high expectations of me, looked at me and said, "What are those wrinkles near your eyes?"

I replied, "Those are my wisdom lines; I have earned them."

Then he looked at me and continued with, "What are those wrinkles by your mouth?"

I looked at him with a bit disdain, replying, "Those are my smile lines; I deserve them!"

Then he had the nerve to say as he pointed at the lines between my brows, "What are those lines?"

Before I realized it, I quickly replied, "Those are my f ### you lines; don't mess with me!"

I do not use the F-bomb often, yet sometimes ... sometimes, that is the only word to use.

After that, he did not know what to say and laughed at me. As he would often say, "If you were as big as your mouth ..." Needless to say, I grew a little bit taller that day.

Just when I thought I had the right answers that day, my daughter came home from school. We chatted as usual and I had to say at one point, "Did I give birth to you to give me a hard time?" We laughed so hard as we continued to chat and I began to tell her, without using names, of a school behavioral issue. She laughed at me as I told her of the situation. She asked me what I thought about the behavior. It was about a child I had to discipline. I call myself the nicest mean guy on campus. I told her, without names, what I choose to do and, "I believe there are no bad students, they just make bad choices."

I thought she was going to fall off her chair. "Are you serious, Mama'?"

And of course I was! She quickly replied, "There are awful students and they deserve what they get!" She knew I was serious with my reply and I didn't miss a beat. I love that she gives me a joyful hard time and keeps me on my toes.

If I am being charged with a fault of being happy and having a different perspective in life, then I strongly believe and I am the first to say, "I am guilty as charged!

♪ ♫ ♪

"Redneck Woman"
Gretchen Wilson

"

*It's good to be loved; it's profound
to be understood.*

"

Ellen DeGeneres

CHAPTER 5

HOUSTON WE HAVE A PROBLEM

Value: Friendship

"I am not asking for anything in particular—just letting you know …

"I'm emailing you from outer space, a place I was sent unintentionally and without directions. I know I can handle any challenge. I am a little lost, yet I will find my way. Without communication, I believe time and patience can fix most any emotional need. I have entered a place way up here. I am not sure where I am or where I go next. It appears as if my mission has ended, yet no notice has been given. I am not quite clear what my task is here.

"I thought this would be a simple mission filled with fun, far beyond the sun. I thought I passed all my pre-tests, yet without confirmation I find myself in doubt. I thought I was going to the stars, yet with one look in my eyes the moon was not far. Little did I know where flight 923 was taking me!

"Aware of what I was doing, unaware of the changes it would bring me. Knowing change and fun was the mission for me; however, I am sitting here asking please. Please tell me how to fill the void that feels so huge. From here, how do I keep that sparkle you so loved?

Tell me how I missed that one important lesson that told me what to do once I got here with no one to share so much with?

"I need to share the beauty that surrounds me and the joy of this journey. Tell me how to get past this feeling of no one being here. There are lessons untold with so much to unfold. Please tell me, Houston, I haven't failed my mission."

This is a note I never mailed to my best friend, a childhood friend who truly knows me. We were a part of the Madison Avenue Brats. He was actually my brother's friend and quickly became my best friend. No, we never dated, yet he was on my front porch waiting after every date I had. He has been there since we were in the 10th grade. I don't know what it was exactly that connected us so. We would talk for hours and I knew there was no drama. Who says you cannot have a best friend of the opposite gender? I am the only girl among six brothers. I was raised with boys all my life. I was really spoiled. I would rather say, really loved! Needless to say I get along very well with the male gender. Yes, I do have several female friends and of course I love "girl time," yet there is nothing like having that one special friend who is with you to the end.

Can you imagine why I would write a note about being on the moon? Well, let me tell you.

Many years of hearing all my chit-chat, he never once said, "Stop talking." He never once said, "No time for you." He laughs at me and with me. He really has been with me through everything. Yes, even after I got married.

In our teenage years we lived in the "pit," a challenged area otherwise known as West Pittsburg, California, We, the Madison Avenue Brats kept each other out of trouble and sometimes in trouble. Fun trouble, that is. It was a place I knew I wanted to get out of. I wasn't sure how I would do that, yet I knew this industrial, high-stress city. My Papa John was like my other dad and he lived in Monterey, California. That was the direction for me. Like split families, I would spend my school year with my mom in the Bay Area and my summers with my other dad in Monterey. After one special visit to Monterey, I came home with an engagement ring on my finger. Was this my way out of West Pittsburg or was I "in love." I believe I was. He was the football captain there and I was a cheerleader at home. Perfect match, right? I thought so. I had known him since I was nine years old, so why wouldn't I believe him when he said, "I will love you forever."

This took place in my freshman year in college. I was still at home in the "pit" with my mom to save money, I was not sure, really, which direction I wanted to go.

I was a cheerleader in high school and college and was getting ready to audition for the San Francisco 49ers' cheerleader team. My fiancé was not happy at all about that. No way was I going to be married and travel with all those football players IF I made the team!

I was at my fork in the road! It was very clear with road signs and all.

Which way was I going to go?

How was I going to make my decision?

What was next?

So guess where I went? You got it, right to my best friend. He always helped me work through everything. Little did I know my brother already told him I was engaged! When I finally got the chance to speak with him, he shocked the crud out of me. He simply said, "What do you really want? What is going to make you happy?"

How did he get so wise? Yet again, he really knew me and more so, he really understood me. At that moment, it hit me like a ton of bricks, straight to my heart. I looked at him and said, "If I got what I really wanted and it would really make me happy … (pause) … you were always so hard-nosed."

He interrupted and said, "If I wasn't so hard-nosed, that would be my ring on your finger." He hugged me with the deepest and most sincere hug I ever felt. We both knew the direction I was going.

At that moment, he sent me to the moon. A place where he kept me protected emotionally and dressed me in a suit of love that would get me through the storms and the elements of life.

I knew going to Monterey, getting married, and getting out of the "pit" was my next move.

Now skip forward many years, like 23, when I made a phone call and said, "Houston, we have a problem."

Still being on the moon emotionally, my best friend was still right there with me. He was on the other end of the phone line and at times was my life line that never failed me. He was with me on the phone through all these years, tears, and joy. His line of business, entertainment, kept him traveling and all so busy. Our lives are very different yet so connected and he is never too busy to stop and check in.

> **" you cannot clap with one hand "**

With this call I explained I was at another fork in the road. This one wasn't so clear, yet had all the signs of a broken heart, broken spirit, and a broken marriage. It was the hardest decision I had to make, since I truly believed in the vows of marriage. I believed "for better or worse," yet I could not compete with a choice that was out of my control. I do know my part in the situation and I also know "you cannot clap with one hand." Of all the lessons life has taught me, I know it takes two to tango.

It takes two to agree or disagree and it takes two to fight. After years of trying to figure it out, what I discovered was he fought with me, not for me. He did not fight for us.

When you truly love someone over something, you fight for them. Not for that something. I have had to really fight with the fact that I was stronger than that and I did not fail. His "that" does not matter, what matters is that was not me he was fighting for.

There is faith in fighting. No one wants to fight in a relationship. I certainly didn't. However, when you discover in the fighting that the fight is not for you that is a battle not worth losing your spirit over.

Many times I have said, "I am so tired of being strong," yet now I find myself saying thank you to him for forcing me to find my strength which helped me weather the storms.

The big bad wolf could not huff and puff and blow the house down. Yet one person in my world with just words took the white picket fence and the lemon tree in the backyard down to the ground.

I thank him, though. I thank him for giving me strength I never knew was in me. It wasn't all bad. I did learn the lesson of the saying,: "When life gives you lemons, make lemonade!"

Starting the process of divorce was heartbreaking, yet we both agreed it was for the best. Neither one of us had a better suggestion. Honestly, I was exhausted from the fight. I had allowed myself to live in a bubble, in a bigger bubble on the Monterey Peninsula. We lived in a very "quant-like" area that I did not leave since I moved out of "the pit." I wouldn't even go across town alone as that frightened me so. Instead of growing once I left "the pit" it was like I entered "his world" and lost a big part of me. Or maybe I just hadn't discovered ME yet.

Pain has always propelled me straight to my purpose.

Don't get me wrong. I did grow. I did learn. I did have some great times and I do believe I got the best part of the marriage. I got two beautiful, incredible kids and priceless lessons I could only have learned by being married.

I knew the next steps in life were going to be tough so I took steps right to New York with my cousin, Sherrie, and dear friend, Leesa. All three of us shared November birthdays and we were going to celebrate life.

I knew going to my best friend was not an option this time because I didn't want my heart to lead the conversation and possibly put more challenges on my plate.

Being on the moon this time actually protected me from myself. At this point, distance was the deal. I needed to figure this out on my own and I felt something big was going to happen. I just didn't know what it was. I was in a place of pain and I felt it to the core of my soul. I knew I had to step back and look at the bigger picture.

I needed my head to guide me and my heart to rest and heal. What better way than "retail therapy," New York-style? Yeah, buddy, three girls in New York! Who knows what kind of plan I would come home with!

We rode in from the airport on the first day in a Yellow Cab with three suitcases inside and autumn leaves in the streets. Nine days later we rode in a white limo in the snow through Central Park back to the airport. What a week, what an experience and what a way to make a plan for what was next.

Going to Ground Zero was surreal.

Seeing the church across the street without even a mark on the steeple was so sweet, and posters lining the fence with messages so deep! It all reminded me that my sorrows were not so big, that

 I too could rise above the loss I was feeling. Experiencing the aftermath of 9/11 has touched us forever, especially as I was hoping this week away from home would give me more strength that I desperately desired.

Conquering the subways to Queens was quite an impressive feat and finding Tiffany's in the snow was nothing short of ter-rif-ic! Seeing the lovely Lady Liberty was utterly breathtaking. Who would believe all the wonderful people we met along the way? We enjoyed many cultures in several cities in seven days. We toasted "opa" with the Greeks in upper Manhattan, sipped wine with the Italians in Little Italy, and did shots of vodka with the Russians in Queens. That is where we were given the nickname, "Die Hard American Women." It was all so incredible, so empowering, and invigorating too!

I remember standing at a street corner waiting for a stoplight as we three girls were laughing hysterically. A woman looked at me and said, "What are you drinking? I want some!" We chatted for a moment as we were waiting for the light to change. She said, "What do you do? Do you have a card?"

My cousin looked at me and quickly said, "What do you do, DiAnna?" She was trying to get me to "own my position" as a new Life Coach! It felt GREAT! It was empowering and helped me to see that my energy really was bigger than me.

New York was the best!

I love billboards and books, signs and doors. They all give you messages if you look and read beyond the words. Sounds silly, yet I was becoming "awake to my life" and I didn't want to miss a thing. There are so many signs in New York and a lot of them spoke to me.

My biggest concern with my choice of divorce was how it was going to affect the family. Would I be "in" or would I be "out?" Would they, my in-laws, still love me as I so deeply love them? By now, my spirit was so broken I could not think of what would come next. I just had to take the steps.

With that I read something so profound: We need not change our lives or interrupt the lives of those around us. Positive changes will simple occur as a result of our growth and understanding. All we need to do is shift the focus of our attention from material reality to spiritual reality, from undue concerns with matter to the love of truth. (Excerpted from: Being on the Path by Astrid Fitzgerald.)

I believe I was on my path. After a long time healing, I once again called my "lifeline." This time it was with joy and a jolly comment when my best friend asked how I was doing. My answer was, "I feel like I am a volcano ready to erupt."

He said, "I thought you were doing better."

 I quickly responded with, "I am. I am not mad. My emotional volcano will not erupt with hot lava; it will erupt with Skittles, a rainbow of joyful colors."

He laughed and said, "Of course it will." And then he said, "She's back," meaning he knew all along I had the strength to do what needed to be done and he was waiting to celebrate the life he felt I was meant to have.

He has always been an "in the moment" type of guy and he reminds me to be the same. I have learned many lessons here on the moon and I hope someday a real good astronaut will take me to the stars as long as I stay focused, and he will navigate his way to me.

I must remind myself of the words I wrote so long ago as I think of my dear friend and his guiding ways: "If we live in the past, it's depression, if we live in the future, it's anxiety. All the more reason to live for today." That's for me this moment and forever!

Friends are priceless and I never take this one for granted. I appreciate, love and admire a gift so graciously given and I pray I am half the friend to him as he has been to me.

♫♪

"Unwritten"
Natasha Bedingfield

"

Make yourself a blessing to someone. Your kind smile or a pat on the back just might pull someone back from the edge.

"

Carmelia Elliot

CHAPTER 6

MAX'S RESTAURANT

Value: Faith

We ran into each other in town and he said, "I must tell you, you saved my life." He continued, "I was so overwhelmed with life and the load of caring for my handicapped child, I just couldn't imagine another day of life. It was YOU who changed my mind from making a terrible choice. I was on my way to your office, and as I was going up the stairs I was thinking, 'After this, I am going to …' I didn't because of you!"

He explained, "You helped me with my daughter's needs and you did it with such spirit and genuine care. Then you said in your kind and gentle way something that changed my mind from any choice I thought I was going to make after leaving your office. Thank you, thank you for being there and being you!"

I do not remember this particular moment in time, as I had helped him many times. He did not share with me the magical words that changed his mind. It really doesn't matter at this point. What matters is that because I helped someone, they are here to tell me that story.

I give it my best shot to help everyone who comes into my office. You really never know how you affect someone unless they tell you. I do believe the words of Mother Teresa, "Let no one ever come to you without leaving better and happier."

I was blessed that, one, he was alive to tell me the story, and, two, in doing what I love to do, I saved the life of another. I do not take that for granted.

I do what I do because I love it. I love working with and helping others. I may be a tiny one, yet I do believe the good Lord blessed me with a big heart.

> **" I may be a tiny one, but I do nothing small. "**

I knew that working in the school was a stable and good-paying job. Yet I also knew my body and soul was telling me I wanted more. What it was, I was not sure.

This was a trying time as I was going through a divorce and trying to get past the feelings of failure.

By this time in my life I had done breath work, sweat lodges, and a lot of therapy. Finding that something to strengthen my spirit was just what I discovered in the midst of a busy restaurant called Max's. Studying to add Life Coach to my plate was the direction for me. The travel it required to go to school and the continued tuition, all represented major issues in my life at that time. I made the decision. I am going to continue it!

My children were close to graduating high school and getting ready for their adult life, and it was time I discovered what was next for me.

What a process, one that changed my world in the middle of Max's restaurant. I discovered my higher power was in me all along and I was not on this journey alone.

It was a beautiful day and all of us students were eager to go to the next level of this occupation called Life Coach.

I had the greatest instructors. They sure knew how to get us in the moment and in the matter. They taught us how to be the client and how to be the coach. We had homework every week and had to have clients with each level. The toughest part of going back to school was trying to keep up with family demands and making sure I did not miss a family event because of school. I was trying to be Wonder Woman. You know, in the movie, her name was Diana!

Two of my most memorable exercises during the course filled me with absolute amazement.

The first was when I was supposed to get a client, follow the instructions of having a conversation on the phone and help that client process the issue at hand. They wanted us to practice phone consultations because it allowed us to expand our clientele. Wouldn't you know it, the person who agreed to be my client for that exercise was not available that night at the last moment? Were they not available or were they not ready to work with their stuff? I will never know, yet I want to thank them for not being available that night because what happened next would not have been possible without them bailing out.

Now, trying to squeeze in my family demands with my schooling, I knew I was going to be challenged this particular weekend because my son had an out-of-town college football game and I was not about to miss his game. He had a good following of family and this game brought my Aunt Ruth and Uncle Allen, who would be seeing him play for the first time. Little did my aunt know how she would play a part in changing my life that night!

She agreed to be my client for my homework. Our "session" was not going to be on the phone; it would actually take place in the car on the drive home in the dark. We all played musical chairs with the cars, as my uncle took their car home and my aunt and I drove home together in my car.

She lived 45 minutes away from the game and that was exactly how long my homework session had to be.

Oh my word! What a session. Everything my instructor told us to do was not possible while focusing on traffic. The time of the session was definitely a challenge. It was 10:30 p.m. by the time we got out of the game (we won!). We were both very tired and it was quite distracting finding our way back to the right route after making a wrong turn. No one ever accused me of having a good sense of direction. Even with all the distractions, we had an in-cred-i-ble session!

I was able to get my aunt to the place my instructor spoke of. I just didn't get there the instructor's way. Now I had to go to class and confess my wrongdoing.

I approached my instructor the next morning early before everyone else got to class and thought for sure I would hyperventilate while trying to tell her I did not do the homework the way she instructed. She looked at me, started clapping her hands, and said, "Yahoo!"

What was going on? What had I said? Certainly nothing that made her upset.

She looked straight at me in the eyes and said, "Did you do the work? Did you complete the exercise? Were you happy with the outcome?"

> " **I invite you to fail forward frequently** "

I answered yes to all of her questions.

She said, "Then your way was not wrong. It was different and I invite you to fail forward frequently."

Those words will stick with me forever.

That experience certainly gave me more confidence in my future sessions with clients.

It really prepared me to be my own best coach and became the second-best experience of my training.

So many times when I am faced with a challenge, I go to my toolbox of tips and experiences of this education and go to work on me. I recall after completing my first level in this course I was in a deep place, still working with the divorce. I called my therapist.

She said, "You know what to do. You know what you would do if a client came to you." She continued, "This is what I want you to do and then get back to me." Her instructions were for me to book an appointment with myself, give myself all the tools I would give a client, bill myself for "work well done" then pay myself. To top it off, go spend that check on myself!

How did she know? That is just what the doctor ordered and it worked! What an empowering process.

Now, this does not happen all the time, yet it sure is my "go to plan," knowing I really am always there for me, myself and I. We are a pretty good team!

I do want to say sometimes, no matter what tools I have in my toolbox of skills, knowledge and experience, I cannot see the answer to what is right under my nose. That is when I have surrendered and sought additional assistance.

I now have had years of experience doing interactive play through coaching. After my introductions when I work with groups or individuals, the first questions that really get their attention are: What is your name? What does it mean? Who named you and why? Tell me the story.

Then I challenge them to discover the beginning of their story. If they don't know, I ask them to get the story and come back in all that energy.

I explain that their name is their virtue and it is their birthright to own that energy!

Now, believe me that is not an easy task. Teaching that, I have had to stand in my own energy and my own story. That in itself has been interesting. I have really had to face my gremlin of shame and embarrassment. Why? Because my dad named me after his championship fighting pit bull. She was coal black and the best in Mississippi.

I was much too young to ever watch a dog fight and besides, I know to the core of my soul I could never watch such an event.

It was the time and the way of the south.

I remember telling a friend how knowing my dad trained and entered this dog into such events has always bothered me. My friend's quick comment was, "Wasn't she a champion? Well there ya' go!"

I never looked at the origin of my name like that until that moment when I was asked to describe who named me and why. Now I honor that energy and at times I even thank that "pit bull" in me for giving me great strength when I need it! Not that I would ever fight to the degree of that dog, yet the metaphor does give me great strength.

I did find myself saying one day, quite loudly, "Don't push me or

I will come out fighting like a pit bull" It was that moment that I knew I was standing in the energy of my given name. However, my bark is certainly bigger than my bite.

Here's the next part of that exercise. What does your name mean? Mine, well, this has been a challenge to accept. My name, DiAnna, means DIVINE. I believe there is only one DIVINE and I always say "I am just DiAnna." I must say I do love saying Diana is also the goddess of the moon.

I love the moon and as humbling as it is, I do embrace my divine-ness.

When I do this exercise with my clients, students, or groups that I work with, it becomes a great joy to see everyone step into their birthright and learn so much about themselves just by discovering more about their name.

With only two classes from completing this level of the coach's course, I knew I still had so much more to learn. This was a tough day in class. Exercises that challenged many of us led us straight to Max's restaurant after class to surrender our day, let go of our emotions and enjoy a meal together.

As we were on our way to the restaurant, one of my classmates ask me straight up, "Do you believe in God and do you want to see the face of Jesus?"

What? Was she pulling my leg or trying to find out what my religious beliefs were? Where did that statement come from? This course was not religious based; however, I do have great faith. I just wasn't expecting a question like that! However, I raised my eyebrows as if to say maybe.

After taking a moment and realizing she was serious and was ready to accomplish that process if I was open, she was on it. Out of curiosity, I thought about allowing her to show me.

As all six of us women squeezed into a booth of a very loud, fun, active restaurant. I still had not answered her. She squeezed in on the other side of the table and at the opposite end from me. We were all talking and ordering drinks as she caught my eye. She mouthed the words, "Do you want to see the face of Jesus?" Before I knew it, she was taking me to a place through words that was the next best thing to a joyride to heaven.

I don't remember what she said, or how long the process lasted. May I remind you this was all happening in the midst of a very busy, loud restaurant? I do remember her facial expressions, her body gestures, and me focusing on her mouth so I could hear her words over all the chaos in the restaurant.

Being in awe and listening to my entire body say, "It's okay, surrender to the process," I looked at her face, saw her eyebrows lift and heard her words, "Yes, that's it, do you see him? Do you see Him?"

Again, I do not remember the process or how long it took; all I know is, I did see the face of Jesus. I saw her face, then it faded into His face. Clear as day, it was Him!

Him being the vision of my God, Him being my inner spirit, Him being a part of my soul! His face is the one I have seen in pictures all my life.

For everyone who has a higher power, I believe they have their own "face" of that power. Some may see it, some may hear it, and some may feel it. Whatever that power is for you and you call it your faith ... I know I have embraced my higher power and my faith has certainly helped me to see all the good in myself, the good in others and good in the world.

How was I so blessed to get such a gift when I never even got her contact information to follow up on what happened? Did I need a follow up? No!

A joyful reminder of my higher power is the rainbow. They say it is God's promise. In my lifetime, I have seen rainbows and sunbows and I am waiting to see a moonbow. Yes, they all exist.

What I discovered in Max's restaurant was nothing short of a miracle in the fact that I surrendered and allowed my soul to surface.

Thank you, Jesus, for seeing my face!

Someone once told me Jesus has three answers to our prayers: One is "Okay," two is, "Not now," and three is "I have something better for you."

I do believe we need to practice patience, for so much is out of our hands.

Faith is friendly, fun and full of surprises. So is the magic of Christmas! As my great grandma Olivia always said, "Those who believe, receive."

I say, "I believe!"

Speaking of Christmas, that is my favorite time of the year. So much magic, so many lights. It certainly fills my heart with so much delight. My kiddos always say, "Momma, what are you going to do with all those decorations?" So many of them in every room.

I simply tell them, "I do it for you." My decorations make me happy, yes, in every room. From a porcelain Santa to a sweet little tin can, one filled with little pieces of paper of our plans for what we would do during our winter break from school when they were children.

A wise old Christmas Santa said it best, "The further away you are from where you started, the closer you get to where you belong. Sometimes you end up right back where you started because that is the place you are supposed to be."

I thought I was supposed to be married. I was actually supposed to be happy and that is where I began in the marriage. Don't get me wrong, I would not change a minute of my decisions while being in the marriage even with all the challenges. I reflect back and thank my "ex" for all the lessons learned. There was love in the relationship, yet not the love that was meant for the two of us. We married very young, at the ages of 19 and 20, and as we grew up we grew apart and found ourselves going in different directions, one I certainly desired, needed, and deserved.

The love he and I shared without a doubt gave me my two greatest gifts and I call them Jacob and Rebecca!

In each class course completed up to this point, I still had no clue where the divorce was taking me and at this point it didn't matter. What mattered was me being able to hold onto to my spirit.

♫ ♪ ♪

"One Moment in Time"
Whitney Houston

"

The strength of a family,
like the strength of an army,
is in its loyalty to each other.

"

Mario Puzo

CHAPTER 7

KATRINA

Value: Loyalty

Now that I had survived the crash of 2004, the crash of the divorce, I didn't think I could take any more. There were days I didn't think my legs would hold me up. Those were the days I would get on the floor and pray like I never had before!

In my world I was fighting a battle I did not know how to fight. I didn't even have the strength sometimes to get out the door. It was exhausting to do such emotional work. Yet it was going to get done and it certainly wasn't fun. I felt like I would never run out of tears.

My beautiful auntie who helped pull me from the edge said some words that will forever stick in my head: "As long as you have tears you will cry, as long as you cry you will live, as long as you live, you can go on". — Auntie Jeanie

I would pray every day "Please, dear Lord, give me the strength ..."

No matter how much I wanted the change in my life, the divorce hurt. It hurt to the core of my soul! It was so painful and I would not wish it upon my worst enemy. It would kill 'em' for sure.

There were days I thought I would die without my spirit.

New York was fabulous, yet as I often thought during our kitchen remodel—oh yeah, did I mention we were going through a complete kitchen remodel during our process of splitting the sheets? My thought was, "New kitchen, same dirty dishes." I could not scrub the pain away, no matter what cleanser I used.

I continued my schooling because that gave me more strength. I felt it was important to keep my mind occupied in the growth of a better me, even if I felt like I was not moving toward that place called happiness fast enough.

Nike brand hit the nail on the head! "No pain, no gain." Boy does that say a lot! This schooling was pain. I had to "bring my stuff" to learn how to get others out of that place.

I needed to continue my schooling for my Life Coach path. I have heard many times you teach what you need to learn.

I sure needed to learn how to see my happiness again, how to hold my happiness in my heart again and how to heal my hurt so my happiness could return. I knew it was in me; I just had to feel it!

I could feel that volcano stirring around, bubbling at times, and I wanted to make sure it was not going to erupt with hot lava.

I had a window to the hallway in my office at work. A little sixth grader walked past the window. He looked in and then came back for a double take. He looked at me with his precious little face and said sincerely, "Are you okay, Ms. G, you don't look like your happy self."

I knew right then I had to get out of that rut that was stealing my spirit.

Just when I thought it couldn't get any worse, it did!

Hurricane Katrina hit my home of Mississippi. Seven family members were affected, yet no one died, thank God! I knew I wanted to do something to help, but what? I was now in a new relationship yet financially on my own and on a tight budget. I could not financially support them in Mississippi. Sitting at my desk, I realized, I am a grief supporter with hospice. I can give them ME!

While planning this trip to Mississippi, my gremlins came to play. What could I do, just little ol' me and my partner-in-joy. He was so like-minded and eager to follow my lead. I call him my partner-in-joy because he brought a lot of my joy at this time into my life. My children were not giving me much joy at this point. They were not happy with this relationship because he was twenty years my junior, yet his soul was every bit my age.

I was told, with anger, "You must be going through a midlife crisis."

My reply was, "I am not going through a midlife crisis, I am going through a midlife celebration. If discovering my happiness is a crisis, bring it on!"

My partner-in-joy and I got on an airplane. Oh, my words, I was going back home again to a place that gave me that "taste of heaven," yet this time it would not be the same.

We got off the airplane in Gulfport, rented a car and drove the coast to get to D'Iberville. That is where my cousins, Tina and R.J., lived. We would be staying with them and helping at my younger cousin Cody's middle school which had been destroyed.

As we made our way, we didn't have a clue as to what awaited us. My partner-in-joy did not say a word; he was as shocked as I was.

My emotions, of course, went deeper with the notion that this was my birth home! He allowed me to sit in deep thought as he drove and without any words, he held the space for me to get to that place of strength and attitude that would soothe the souls of so many hurting hearts.

Katrina took so much away! That meant it took a part of ME away. I discovered not only did it harm several of my family member's homes, it also destroyed the hospital I was born in, the home I once lived in and the Waffle House where I used to eat waffles.

Could I do it, had I learned enough? Were he and I going to make it through this week? This was our first time traveling together since we connected. Did I know him enough to trust the relationship and to do what was needed to be done in such a place of disaster and dismay?

I recall coming around the corner to the coast as we were driving from the airport. It was like we entered a war zone. I could not believe my eyes. My heart stopped and I could barely breathe, thinking, "I just got my dad back." How could this take so much away? It didn't take him, he was still my dad, yet the roots that grew me were damaged, some destroyed.

Driving along the damaged coastline, we saw only foundations of buildings, roots from trees on the beach, boards from the lifeguard towers in the streets and not a single soul out and about. I never imagined a war zone, yet I was in the midst of the biggest one my thoughts could ever imagine.

> **Yes, your project is bigger than you, yet not bigger than your energy!**

Still driving along the coast, I caught myself facing that gremlin of "being enough" and I went back to the classroom in my mind. I recall going to my instructor, telling her I wanted to do this trip and what my project was for the week. I looked at her in great concern and said, "I think this project is bigger than me!"

In her wonderful wit she quickly responded, "Yes, your project is bigger than you, yet not bigger than your energy!" I remember those words as they gave me the confidence I needed to assure myself that this was a part of those "SKITTLES" ready to erupt from my emotional volcano. My feeling of something BIG. I could feel it in my soul; something colorful and yummy was going to happen.

This is something bigger than me, the loyalty and my love for my birth home. If I could do just a little something to make their lives better for a brief moment in time, then that is where I was going to put my big energy. The loyalty to love others and to accept love is bigger than any energy on earth. I do believe with love and loyalty anything is possible and no hurricane can take that away!

I did not know if I could emotionally go back to my birthplace and connect on a level that was needed to accomplish the outcome I desired. Giving hope and belief to fifth through eighth grade students who had lost their homes, their schools and in some cases, their family required BIG shoes to step into.

Who was I to go back there empty-handed? Did I have any right to share my thoughts and feelings, let alone teach them or think for one moment I could make them "happy" in a time of such great despair?

I asked myself, "Will I be enough?" I had to be my own best coach and say to myself, "You can take the girl out of the South, yet you cannot take the South out of the girl." With that, I hoped I would be enough just being me.

My partner-in-joy and I spent an entire week doing grief work through interactive play. The first day we arrived, as I entered the first classroom of seventh graders (tough age), I truly had no clue what my first words were going to be. Who wanted to start with that boring line "I am so and so from …?" No, I knew I had to get their attention in the first 30 seconds or I was toast!

On my way to that classroom I found a pink plastic Easter egg. I stopped, picked it up, found it "empty," yet filled with so much love, my love. My love for what I do and the love that many of the children so desired. That was going to be my introduction.

I walked into the classroom and the counselor did indeed introduce me as DiAnna from California.

I then said, "Do you really know who I am?" A little boy said "Yes, you are that lady from California."

I then said, "No, I am your neighbor who was born and brought to my home on Santini Street. I am the cousin to your fellow classmate who lost your school. I am Sissy, originally from Mississippi."

I continued by holding up the empty pink egg and saying, "Look what I found. Someone missed this during an Easter egg hunt. It appears empty right?"

They all said, "Yes."

I said, "No, it is filled with something that all of you will get by the end of the week. Are you ready to play and find out what is inside?"

I got 'em' in that first 30 seconds. It was enough to start our journey to a place where I would never be the same after all the discoveries I made in giving enough of me to be enough for them!

The one comment I will treasure forever came from a boy in one of the activities. I recall working with probably the biggest boy in the class. He surely towered over me!

He was determined not to laugh in the activity we were playing. He couldn't hold it anymore. He started laughing so hard and as I approached him he was holding his tummy, laughing hysterically. I asked him, "Does it hurt so good, or does it hurt so bad?"

He replied loudly and with joy, still laughing and holding his tummy as if in pain, "It hurts so good!"

It was all over; they had me by the heart strings. By the end of the week and playing with over 500 students, doing grief work through interactive play was the game of the day. I received many funny looks because most of them were bigger than me. Their expressions of joy and appreciation gave me all I needed to realize my education was not taken in vain.

I take nothing for granted and I am so grateful for opportunities like these to heal my own heart.

This same boy came running up to me as I was leaving the office on the last day, saying, "I am so happy I caught you." He thanked me and said, "You are not that lady from California, you are the laughing lady." I knew what I was doing was right and was enough!

That was a moment in time that no hurricane can destroy. That is called LOVE. Love for mankind, love for family and love for life. Nothing can take that away.

That moment in time for me was worth every moment in school, every moment of concern of being enough, and every moment of precious memories that has guided my journey.

"Mississippi Girl"
Faith Hill

"

The good you do today, will often be forgotten. Do good anyway.

"

Mother Teresa

CHAPTER 8

T.A.S.K. – THE STORY

Value: Kindness

It is true that we teach what we are supposed to learn—not only as a certified teacher yet also as a heart-invested teacher of life.

I love to learn and I keep asking myself, what is it I am supposed to teach?

I do believe I have discovered it. KINDNESS!

Kindness to me is not just giving or doing for someone; it is sharing the soul. That is when it is truly felt. That is when it is truly known.

Mark Twain says it so beautifully ~ "Kindness is the language which the deaf can hear and the blind can see."

That is kindness to me. That is what I want to see. That is what I want to teach the world to feel. How will I do that? I will have to see!

One of my favorite comments when I am working with students in a negative situation is, "Only kindness speaks." They know I am not asking them to hold back their feelings; I am teaching them to get out of that negative pull. I am asking them to remember "only kindness speaks" loud enough for others to hear even when you whisper.

Trying to be kind and gentle with myself while still feeling the divorce, I knew I had to get out of my bubble and explore, discover and engage more in my own community. Before I could grow and learn I needed to know what was in my own backyard.

What is beyond my "mommy joy" of getting my own children through high school, what is beyond the divorce, and what is next in my life?

That is when I heard of a community program called Leadership of Monterey Peninsula. I loved the mission statement and I loved the purpose of the program. This might be the next step for me.

I remember my interview with the board and discussing my playful essay. No way were they going to pick me … and they did! Now that I was in the program, what was I going to do?

It was a nine month program that focused on our own community issues with a different theme/subject each month such as juvenile justice, agriculture, health, and six other themes. In the mornings we would hear from a panel of professionals in that particular area, then the afternoon would be spent in the field of that area.

There were about 45 students in the program. The instructor began telling us in the first meeting, in addition to our field work we would also have to develop our own community project that was long-standing and self-sustaining. She explained how we would have to split into groups, assess our community needs, develop a project, be creative, and then put it into motion by the end of the year. We could develop anything we felt the community could use and she repeated, "Be creative." She did not end her instructions until she added, "Each group needs a leader."

Oh my goodness, the gremlins came to play.

What did I have to offer? What topic would I choose? Who would want to be in my group if I chose to be a leader? All those gremlins came to play!

The instructor told us to think about what we would want to do. She instructed us to take a morning break, think about it, and when we returned we would then break into groups. This being our first day, holy moly, talk about divine intervention. This community was going to get the best from the best mishmash of people who had not even officially met each other yet.

Everyone in this class was a born "leader" in the community whether we knew it, acknowledged it or had not yet discovered it. That is why we were drawn to or were invited into the program.

During the entire morning break I felt like a scared little school girl who was worried about being "picked." Who would want me on their team?

After the break we all came back together. The instructor asked if any of us came up with a project idea or area of interest. Four of us raised our hands. Did I really do that? I was actually one of the four who raised our hands, thinking, for sure many others would raise their hands Nope, only four of us.

Not sure why only four out of 45 of us raised our hands! What was up with this group? Many "followers" not yet ready to brave the "leader" role? Was I brave or just crazy thinking I could do this?

I knew I wanted to do a youth project and I was concerned if I didn't raise my hand I would give up my opportunity to discover what that feeling inside me was. What was calling me? Was this my opportunity for my "volcano of Skittles" to erupt, to color my world with joy? I did not know and was I brave enough to raise my hand and take the lead? Putting all fear aside, I did just that!

When did I get brave enough to raise my hand and be leader of one of the four groups? Who is this person going through a divorce, working full time and still trying to be the focused momma I wanted to be? Hoping that I was not losing the light that shone so bright at one time. Hoping this program would ignite that light.

The instructor split the room into four groups: 1) Health for elders 2) Hunger in the community 3) Agriculture and 4) The youth, which was my group.

I had no clue at that moment what to do, yet I knew I wanted to develop a youth project.

Long story longer … during the break I thought, beyond the fear of raising my hand and voicing my thoughts, who would really come to my project? Yet at this point in my life I knew I had to face my fears and just hope that my decisions would lead me to learn just what was waiting for me to teach.

I knew going into a youth project would put me in an area I was a very familiar with since I had done Challenge Day and Youth to Youth for several years while working at the middle school. I thought, "I might have some ideas to share."

To my complete surprise, 14 people came to my corner. We had a group, yahoo!! Developing a group is a challenge in itself. How many chefs are in the kitchen? We will soon find out.

Discovering everyone's strengths and weaknesses was the first step after we brainstormed the purpose in the project. I knew my weakness was asking for money. Do we have a tax collector in the group? Someone who doesn't think twice about asking for money?

I remember saying at one point, "If I had Oprah's money, I would be dangerous!" Dangerous because I would give to so many charities, dangerous because I would want to change the world, in a good way.

Using the word "dangerous" simply means I would probably harm my own heart in the face of feeling like I was not doing enough or not having the strength to protect my heart from many who would just want the money.

If I had Oprah's endless funds what would my world look like? What would it feel like? Since having very little money has always been an issue in my life, I find myself having a hard time asking for money from anyone. I do know to complete any type of charitable project, I will need money. How will I lead a group that needs money if I cannot ask for it? How will I do that if I don't face my fears of asking for money and help! Are those the lessons I need to learn?

The more I think of the statement, "If I had Oprah's money," the more I realize her greatest wealth is not in all her money. I believe it is in her wisdom, her experience and her contacts!

> Don't pray
> For money,
> pray For the
> means to make
> the money!
>
> – Great Grandma
> Olivia

Yes, I believe CONTACT IS IMPACT. If only I had some of her contacts I could make much more impact.

I certainly would be able to make many more dreams come true for others, starting with me.

A grant writer said to me, "Money is the mother's milk of the world." We need the money to make it all happen. To birth a project we call "our baby," we must have that milk.

Oprah makes it all look so easy. However, I know she works very hard and passionately to make it happen for those in her path. I would love to be in her path. Since I am not, I will certainly learn from her as a role model.

I will hold close in my heart what my great grandma always said about money. "Don't pray for money, pray for the means to make the money happen." She was a very wise woman and I always pray for the means as I am not afraid of work.

With that, I knew being the leader of this youth project would be a lot of joyous work.

I also knew it would challenge me to every ounce of my soul.

Now we had our group and we had our plan. We worked for a couple of weeks developing a youth mentoring program and connected with a local non-profit that had an after school program which helped students with doing homework, learning values, and developing goals and skills for their future.

I was so impressed with what we came up with, I asked my group if they would mind me taking some thoughts into the school and see what would happen. They agreed and T.A.S.K. was born. This being a nine-month program, I was hoping to birth a project that would color my world.

I went to school and interviewed 21 middle school students with the request that they stay with me through the end of the year as we completed our project. Seventeen sixth, seventh and eighth graders made the commitment. We agreed to meet once a week during lunch and we also switched up what my adult group was doing.

The students and I decided we wanted to complete four projects by the end of the school year: One school project, one community project, one county project and one international project.

I went back to my big group and they were actually amazed that the students wanted to be a part of the bigger project. I was pretty impressed myself. Knowing the students' direction, the adults were even more amazed.

I called the students "the cherubs" because I believe every child is an angel. They became more excited each week we met.

My big group met every other week after work and my T.A.S.K group met once a week during lunch.

Every week I would ask the cherubs, "What does T.A.S.K. mean to you? "I had originally called it "task" because it was my task to get through the year. To them, I said we needed to "name it, own it, be it." What was that "it"?

They were so excited to go to the white board and brainstorm. Many versions came up for the acronym, yet one stood out...

T.A.S.K. — Together Achieving Successful Kindness.

... I added, for fun, with "Terrific Awesome Sensational Kids." They told me they were "young adults," not kids. We all laughed and T.A.S.K. was born! Definitely a labor of love!

They owned it. The cherubs were so excited they were a part of something bigger. The first of our four projects was our community project. We worked with Caltrans to put in a five-way crosswalk in a very busy part of town. Second came the county project; we worked with the county shelter for homeless men and women. The third was our school project and involved planting a red rose plant during Red Ribbon Week, the big national drug awareness program. The rose represented a drug free zone in the back of the school by the lunch tables. For the international project, we decided to connect hearts and communities. We arranged for the entire Home Economic department to take a week out of their scheduled plan and make hemp friendship bracelets with two red hearts on them, for me to take to Nicaragua on my first out-of-country travel with my Rotary Club.

The project has certainly gone through changes and growth over the years, yet stays the same sweet little child. As all the cherubs have gone through the program, they have changed. I know I have grown and the program is flying to the moon!

It started out at age one: T.A.S.K., a lunchtime club. At age 3 it became T.A.S.K. for Teens. At age 7: T.A.S.K. 4 U & Me. And at age 10: T.A.S.K. 4 U & Me Foundation, Inc.

Receiving our 501-©-3 statutes certainly strengthened my ability to ask for that "mother's milk of the world."

T.A.S.K. was born and I became a member of Rotary. My club was doing an assessment trip for a possible international project and our bracelets would go through that door of opportunity. I was just a baby in Rotary and I had no clue what was in the future for me and T.A.S.K.

I took 100 bracelets, made by the students at school, to an orphanage called Los Quinchos in San Marcos, Nicaragua. It was nothing short of a-maz-ing! I brought many pictures back for my cherubs and they all came to understand the meaning of "the gift of receiving as you give." By the end of the school year, we all, both my big group of adults and my little group of cherubs, learned so much on how giving to others and the

act of kindness leads to something so much bigger than us.

One great lesson I learned in both groups is take time to discover the purpose in the project. This little group certainly met the demands of my instructor. We were curious, captivating and creative. We accomplished just what was required to complete this adult, community-based program at a middle school level. I was so proud of my cherubs!

I may be a tiny one but I do nothing small! I hope and believe in everything I set my heart to and I dream even bigger. Any time I think that I am not reaching high enough or dreaming big enough, I remember the great words of Harriet Tubman: "Every great dream begins with a dreamer. Always remember, you have within you the strength, patience, and the passion to reach for the stars to change the world."

Can I change the world? My little group of cherubs did at one busy street corner that had no crosswalks. We did at a homeless shelter as we served food and had conversations with the men and women. We did as we planted that red rose for a drug free zone, knowing it would grow and be a living symbol of "being drug free is the place to be." And we did change the world with every new friend as we truly "connected hearts and communities" in Nicaragua.

My big group graduated at the end of the year with many connections as mentors to our local non-profit and my cherubs ended our school year knowing they "rocked it." They "named it" they "owned it" and they "became it." We did indeed change the world just by being who we were as we discovered our special gifts in the world. We all Together Achieved Successful Kindness!

As said with humor, joy and great passion by a huge heart of kindness, none other than Ellen DeGeneres, "We need more kindness, more compassion, more joy, more laughter." I definitely want to contribute to that."

I echo her, and aspire to touch hearts and souls as she and Oprah both have done in our world. Without their funds, without their contacts, I will continue one step at a time in my own little way!

♪♫♪

"Happy Girl"
Martina McBride

"

*And those who were seen dancing
were thought to be insane by those
who could not hear the music.*

"

Friedrich Nietzsche

CHAPTER 9

HE DANCED IN

Value: Connection

Imagine feeling a spark of energy as you walk into a room, not knowing what it is or who it is until you discover it.

There is a famous poem that states "people come into your life for a season or a reason..." We may ask, why is that? What is their purpose? Why, why, why?

We may never know why, yet the experience, if you are awake to it, is unbelievable.

I do not know the reason, and it wasn't for a season. Yet in an eight week period I had a glorious experience and the magical opportunity of being awake to just what that poem speaks of.

He danced into my life and exquisitely danced out, just like that! What a beautiful soul! What a beautiful experience!

I signed up for a summer ballroom dance class and was concerned with two issues: one, does height make a difference (remember, I am 4'8" tall) with a dance partner, and two, being single, having to open myself up and allow a connection.

He danced in, danced around and danced in total presence.

Kyle was 6-feet tall, a happy, intriguing, glorious, joyful, present soul who walked into the dance class. I instantly felt his incredible energy.

In body he was maybe 22 years seasoned; his soul, however, had to have had far more years of playfulness.

> " He danced in danced around and danced in total presence. "

As the opening music started, the instructor called out, "Make eye contact with someone and get a home base partner."

His eyes met mine, he picked me! The moment he embraced my hand, he embraced my soul! He looked into my eyes and held the space.

The dance instructor told us when you connect with a partner, you will know it. When Kyle held the space, I knew!

Over the eight weeks of dancing the connection became stronger. It was not lust, it was a connection.

The students would switch partners throughout the night and when my eyes met his, no words were needed. Oh my words, how we danced.

It was not an issue that he was more than six feet of pure joy and playful happiness and I was "energetically tall." We were perfectly matched in many senses of the word.

For weeks we just danced without saying a word to each other. We shared many smiles and when we danced I did not see or hear anyone else in the class. It wasn't until the instructor would say, "Gentlemen down," or, "Ladies move," and like graceful angels the energy in our hands flowed to the tips of our fingers as we separated till our next meeting.

It wasn't until the fifth week that any words were shared. Then it was just a few, yet enough to know we had a connection.

He was wearing a green African t-shirt and I watched that energy dance around the room all night. I wasn't sure how I would break the ice other than just saying to him at the end of the evening, "Hey you, I noticed your t-shirt and had to ask, have you been to Africa?"

He answered with a childlike sweet smile as if to say thank you for asking. "Yes, I worked on a water purification project."

Without thinking, I said, "And you are a humanitarian too." We shared small talk with another student in class and I asked them both what they were studying. Joel said medicine and Kyle said consciousness. I then said to him with a smile, "Of course you are."

He smiled and we went our separate ways as class was over for the night. Oh, how I wanted to hear more. I was so intrigued and amazed with the gifts and energy of such a wonderful soul.

With two more weeks left of class, I wanted to know as much as I could about this fabulous footwork that was attached to someone you would think was an illusion. He danced in late most nights and quietly left without a word.

He must have gone on vacation because he was not at the next class.

That evening was not the same. Of course I enjoyed the class, yet the energy was different. Something was certainly missing. With him not being there, it really gave me the opportunity to look deeper into my thoughts to figure out the "it" that was missing. How can a person make such a difference with it not being a sexual thing!

I could not contain my excitement of discovering the "it" in our dancing. With only one more class session left, I went home and could not get him off my mind. What was this energy? Would he think I was silly by sharing my feelings with him?

I didn't want the wrong impression to be relayed, since I stumble and get stuck when I share words from the heart.

I know I had to step out of that vulnerable place, suck up the fear of how he might respond and just put it out there! I had to share what I was feeling.

I definitely lost sleep over the problem of how to approach such incredible energy and not say something that would embarrass me or him, especially with the age difference. I would not want him to think I was a cougar on the prowl!

This was Monday and I knew I would have to be in the moment and totally present when I stood in front of him next, which would be on Wednesday.

All day Tuesday I went over the words I wanted to share. For the past seven weeks, we had shared few words yet touched the cores of our souls through our eyes.

After many hours of thinking it through, I let it all go and decided, "It is what it is" If he is indeed tuned in to that energy, I will know.

Who was I not to share my thoughts? There was nothing to lose and I prayed I would have the words that would not turn him away. At this point I figured I would or I would not discover this awakening to a connection that very few are able to tap into, and honor the space and the miracles of the moment.

This being our last class, I knew if I did not share my thoughts I would shortchange myself as well as miss acknowledging his gifts, and isn't that what we are all here for, to share peace, joy, love and laughter?

Who knew, after sharing my thoughts he might get a lot of laughs.

Whatever the outcome, I was ready to risk my vulnerability and put it out there.

As everyone was entering class, I walked in and saw him across the room. He was early this night. My heart was pounding, hoping I would not say something that would make me look like a complete ditz or embarrass myself. As I strolled over he caught my eye and smiled.

I approached him and said, "So, how are you?"

He smiled that childlike, playful smile and said, "Great." Of course he was!

I then said, "So are you from around here?"

His smile grew bigger and he said, "Yes, P.G."

I said, "Really!"

Again with a huge smile, he said, "Yes, I went to P.G. High."

I then said in shock, "Really? I work at P.G. High."

He giggled and said, "I graduated in 2006."

I replied, "I was working at the middle school that year."

Then he said "Mrs. Gamecho!?!"

With a raised eyebrow and a burst of laughter, I said "Oh my words—yes!"

We both laughed and I then became very embarrassed, realizing I had connected with one of the past students! I instantly thought: Did that, could that, would that change that magical connection?

We laughed some more and did some small talk and after that initial "oh my words" moment I quickly sucked up the embarrassment and said, "I am not a cougar on the prowl, I wanted to share with you how intrigued and in awe I am of your gift of pure presence. How I am so happy to see someone of your years to be so in tune, so grounded and so present. It warms my heart to literally see the shift in the world. You are so conscious and so present and you hold the space like I've never witnessed before in someone so youthful."

He replied with a soft whisper, "Thank you," and a smile that made him glow angelically.

We both continued to laugh as we heard the teacher say, "Let's go, ladies and gentlemen."

We got into two separate lines to do our warm-ups, me behind him and thinking during the entire time, "Really DiAnna, you are Ms. Gamecho from school." I couldn't help but laugh under my breath endlessly. I just knew after that conversation this last evening could be very awkward.

The instructor then called, "Get your home base partner."

He turned around. I froze. He made eye contact, knotted his forehead as if to say "yep" and gave me a sweet grin. Still frozen, in my mind I shouted, Yahoo!" I hadn't made a ditz of myself! Or if I did, he laughed it off.

Putting myself out there and saying what I thought had indeed turned out to be a relief and a reward.

The instructor called the dance and said, "Now dance." If she only knew what those words meant at this moment.

No one in that room knew exactly what dance was being shared at this time. As our eyes met, the music of life began. There were no words, yet our eyes kicked off the dance of a lifetime. Did I mention, we were doing the waltz?

How could this be possible? How was I so lucky to be so awake to that moment? Why was I so blessed with crossing paths with energy of pure happiness that lit up the room with a light of joy, peace, and so much confidence that I could do this dance? That is just what we did!

It was like being in a dream. To do the moves flawlessly, never taking our eyes off each other. Hearing only the music from our souls.

Oh my words, I could not believe this moment and the energy. The power between two people that spoke the universal language of pure joy, pure love for life. And it showed in our dancing! What fun!

Then it happened. The music stopped. The dance was over and the instructor said, "Gentlemen down."

Kyle and I looked at each other in this realm of the world and knew something special just happened. It is called "the miraculous, magical moment" of being present at all levels in the moment. That is when you dance the dance of life and you are living in that moment!

We switched partners.

At that point I could not wait for our turn again. I did enjoy dancing with the others, yet that connection, that energy, was not there.

Then it happened again. The instructor said, "Back to your home base partner." She called a dance that I was not confident with and hoped that I could hold the space.

As he reached for my hands and our eyes connected, I lost it! I got into my head and stumbled my feet. We laughed and tried again. Then he stumbled and we laughed. Then he said, "Don't think about it, just dance." Oh my words, as I shook it off I looked into his eyes and we danced!

I felt like we were performing in front of thousands with the energy, the music, and the pure joy that was in each twirl, each cuddle and every crossover. We danced and laughed and danced some more!

It is so true, when you let everything in life go and just be in the moment, that is where you live, that is where you find joy and that is where true happiness is found.

When class was over I told him how honored I was to cross his path and how beautiful I thought his path was. I wished him much luck in his travels and offered him my business card to keep in touch. Or if he was back in town and wanted to practice his twirls, he was welcome to email me or call. We both laughed.

One of the other guys standing near us asked if it was okay to hug me. I said with a smile, "You just have to ask."

Then Kyle said, "I'm asking." Oh my words, what a hug! Again no words, just pure connection. Yum!

As I was leaving I turned and looked at him with his breathtaking eyes and said, "You're pretty special, Kyle."

> "
> Have you ever
> danced before
> and what is
> your goal for
> the class?...
> "

And with his childlike grin and so much energy shining all around him, he said, "So are you!"

I felt like an angel had danced into my life and just like that he danced his way into the world.

The first week I walked in the dance class I never imagined walking out on the last night with the experience and opportunity of a lifetime. The opportunity to share and be a part of the shift. Being awake to the moment, that truly is exactly what they speak of in the poem: People come into your life for a reason or a season.

So what is the reason? Do we really have to know? Does it really matter after an experience like this one? Do I ask what lesson, besides dance, was learned here? No, just enjoy it and be grateful for the opportunity and the experience.

At the beginning of the class in the few words we did share, I remember asking him, "Have you ever danced before and what is your goal for the class?"

With his priceless smile he answered, "I want to be a better leader and I want to do that twirl thing."

I returned the smile and thought—"too cute."

He then asked, "Have you danced before and what is your goal?"

> "
> ... I want to be
> a better leader
> and I want to
> do that
> twirl thing.
> "

With a vulnerable smile I replied, "I have not done this dance before and I want to learn to be a better follower."

I believe we both met our goals.

I believe Kyle danced into my life to confirm goodness, pure joy, love for life, and to share the gift of dance. I am more blessed because of this incredible soul, and the dance.

What is "it"? This is it...the purest, deepest love on earth. When two souls are able to tap into, and connect at the core level, these are the moments and this is the dance.

That is the love we were put on this earth to share, to give and to receive. Love is not always sexual; it is the connection between two souls.

When you experience that, you have experienced living life and in that miraculous magical moment you can say, "I have felt the love for life."

Now go look for and embrace every miraculous magical moment you can and dance!

♪ ♫ ♪

"Opening"
John Astin

"

Some people grumble because roses have thorns, I am thankful thorns have roses.

"

Elaine Buchner

CHAPTER 10

THE ART OF HAPPINESS

Value: Gratitude

Picture this, being so close to His Holiness, the Fourteenth Dalai Lama, that you can see the marks on his arm. Yes, it is true, I was that close to him and in absolute awe of his pure presence.

Many times I have heard people say to me, "Are you always this happy?" or, "I want what you are drinking."

I chuckle, then I say, "Yes, most of the time I am this happy," and "This is some strong water."

I have thought for years even through my darkest times, "Why do some people have such a hard time seeing others being happy or sharing in their happy moments?"

It is not that hard to be happy IF you truly feel it in the core of your soul. It must just be a part of you.

That seems to be the only answer I can come up with because so many find it to be a job or a challenge to even discover that "yummy-ness".

What is yummy-ness, you ask? It is my own way of expressing the ultimate goodness in something. Think of it as your favorite something, a pie, a cookie, your best friend. It is that scrumptious yummy feeling in your tummy when you think of taking that first bite or getting that long overdue hug from your friend. Everyone knows that feeling when you say it is so "yummy". Just the thought alone makes you happy.

Sometimes that yummy energy just exudes from me and I don't even realize it till someone brings it to my attention. Then I am humbled and grateful that it is recognized. I can't always explain where it comes from, other than the soul.

In the midst of a very challenging moment, I found myself looking at the person opposite me thinking to myself, "You must not be a very happy person. Happy people just don't treat others like this!"

I certainly was challenged to keep my spirit strong and not take on the energy so desperately trying to take me down.

Unbeknown to me, there was someone watching the situation who approached me shortly after it was all over. He looked at me and said, "Do you ever get mad"?

I gave him a puzzled look and quickly responded, "No, I don't get mad I get hurt. What I do with that hurt is a whole other story".

He looked at me, smirked and, raised his eyebrows as if to say, "I'll bet!"

Being happy is not a job for me, it is my way of life. I am not saying I am always happy. I am saying it is a choice to stay in my happy place.

When I have to decide to be mad and allow that energy to run the situation or to look at the situation in a more positive, productive view, I choose to stop and ask myself—what is the lesson I am supposed to learn right now?

It is not always that easy. Sometimes, I must say, it is hard as heck to keep my chin up, yet I choose happiness every time. I choose to keep the happy adrenaline flowing. I choose not to allow that toxic cortisol (stress chemical) in my soul. That is poison to the soul. I try as often as possible. I am not saying I never get mad, sad, or hurt. I do. When I do, I honor it.

I sit down with it and then I choose to get up one more time. This has not always happened. I have had to allow and accept a lot of awareness and honor the anger. I am so grateful for that something in my soul that keeps me looking to the higher road. I have been accused of living in a fantasy world. When I first heard that comment, I didn't know how to take it. Then I heard it by the same person many times and it was always when I was choosing my happy place versus going to an ugly place.

When I was going through my Life Coach courses, "building your fantasy world" was an actual exercise to teach us how to be in our true "happy place." It was then I no longer took what I thought was an insult. Instead, I actually used it as a tool and a gift to myself as strength to heal and truly be happy.

You never know where life takes you and if you are open and

willing to go with the joys and opportunities that present themselves, you just might find those magical moments that, for me, I never could have dreamed of.

Out of the blue one of my dear friends called me at work and said, "Do you want to go to Colorado and see the Dalai Lama with me?"

I was without words and that doesn't happen often. I replied, "What, really?" I have always wanted to see him and attempt to get as close to the happiest soul ever. Is he real? Is he human? What is he really like?

So many questions, yet no expectations. We were excited to go. I have discovered in life, if whatever you are doing seems to be a battle, fighting one thing or another—such as airline tickets, booking a room, etc.—then it is not meant to be. Yet if it all flows and everything is perfectly in sync, well then guess what? It is meant to be! For me and my friend, there was not a battle to confront when it came to the trip to Colorado, and the experience remains in my memory as phenomenal.

I was surprised how financially reasonable the entire trip was, which made it even better.

So many times we save forever, stress till the day comes to leave and then stress during the trip for everything that should have been done at home.

Not us. We saw the opportunity one day and was on the airplane in less than a week. Talk about spontaneous, that was us and the planning was absolutely flawless.

Arriving at the hotel we quickly discovered we were named "the girls from California" as we actually were the only ones at this event from California. The morning consisted of a full lecture, panel discussion, and mix 'n' mingle. The Dalai filled the afternoon with pure happiness and life lessons I take with me daily.

I had no clue what I would really achieve, believe or accomplish by participating in such an event.

Let me tell you!

Sometimes I say, "Call me gullible Gamecho." I know I am very naïve. This fault was actually a mask of innocence as I walked into the conference room and chose my seat. Looking around the room I saw many different cultures, many different styles, and many men in black.

I seriously laughed to myself, thinking, "How cool is this?" It felt like we were in a movie. We were not. We were in an awesome conference with the topic being discussed the difference between faith and science. Just because you can't see it, doesn't mean it isn't real or doesn't exist. And why does it, if this is so?

The conference room was filled with many people with great minds and occupations. We were just two girls from California who wanted to see the Dalai Lama. We had no true idea of what we had gotten ourselves into.

It was an amazing panel split between religious greats and scientific brilliance. The panel representing faith consisted of a rabbi, a Catholic priest and a spiritual leader. On the opposite side of the table, representing science, was a scientist, a specialist of quantum physics and an atheist. It was an eye-opening, mind-boggling and remarkable open conversation.

The questions and observations that came from the audience made me wonder what I was doing there. I had never been amongst such brilliant people. Yet in the same thought, my level of gratitude flowed beyond the moon.

As the morning progressed it was quite clear that we were right where we were supposed to be. I asked myself, "Why are we here?" I did not know at the moment, yet I was like a deer in the headlights, curious about what was next.

As the men in black kept scoping out the room and talking into the communication devices attached to their ears, I was still naïve to their purpose other than thinking, "The Dalai must be in the house".

I suddenly felt a poke in my side. My friend Lisa said, "Look! Look who that is!"

"What?"

She said, "Look, two seats up and three over to the left."

Oh my words! We were studying with the one and only Steven Spielberg. How did this happen, how did we get to study with Steven Spielberg?

It was now time for a break. The leader of the conference

announced, "This is not just a break but an opportunity to meet and greet and get to know each other and ask questions of each other. Come back knowing each other better than when break first began. Discover something new."

I remember walking out to the hallway, not knowing where I was going other than looking for the little girl's room. It was a long hallway and there were many men in black everywhere. What was happening? Who was here? Was the Dalai really at a level of protection that I needed to look over my shoulder just because I was there? Who knew? I really didn't care since I knew I really wanted to see him and that was all that really mattered. I did feel safe and most definitely in my "happy space."

I did indeed meet many wonderful people during that break and enjoyed some delicious food prepared for all us participants. The more I spoke to those brilliant minds and those spiritual souls, the more I ask myself, "How did I get here?"

Finding my way back to the conference room, I was walking down the hall and saw two people sitting together but doing their own thing: A woman talking on her phone and a man looking at his phone as if to say "I really do not want to answer this phone." His head was down and I could tell his mind was spinning.

As I got closer, I realized it was him ... Steven Spielberg himself. My heart started pounding and I really wanted to say, "Hey." Yet who was I to disturb him by saying hello? Then I had "that moment," the voice in me that said, "YOU ARE YOU and YOU deserve this moment and he deserves to meet YOU!"

Without pausing for a moment I walked right up to him, put my hand out to shake and said, "Hey, I am DiAnna from California, nice to meet you." He chuckled, put his hand out to shake and said, "Nice to meet you."

… And that was it. I smiled and said, "Have a beautiful day." He smiled right back and without a word, put his phone in his pocket and followed me back into the conference room.

Oh my words, I thought my heart was going to beat out of my chest! If nothing else came of this conference, gratitude sure did. Gratitude toward my dear friend for inviting me to such an incredible event. Gratitude for the time together with such a dear person, gratitude for the opportunity to meet so many phenomenal souls. And gratitude for the opportunity to discover my own voice and my own strength to encourage myself to make myself known to someone so big in the world. Even if he just laughed and said hello.

I had made him smile at that moment.

Now it is time to go into the big lecture forum to hear His Holiness, the Fourteenth Dalai Lama.

The forum filled up quickly and I could not believe how we got to sit in the third row from the stage. How did this happen, how did we get so lucky? I turned and looked around the forum and just kept asking myself, "How did we get so lucky?" I don't even remember how or who guided us to those seats; all I knew was that I could see the stage without someone bigger than me blocking the view.

Then it happened. The lights went out, the forum went dark and it felt like they were going to announce, "Elvis is in the building." Instead the announcer said, "Help me to welcome His Holiness, the Fourteenth Dalai Lama".

An energy came over the forum like no other. It was a feeling of pure peace, pure joy, and certainly a lot of happiness!

He was a tiny man who walked from behind the curtains to the center of the stage with a beautiful garment on and a smile bigger than life itself!

A wave of unbelievable emotions came over me, some I could not even begin to explain. Then the tears of pure gratitude for being right where I was at that moment took over. I could not hold them back. As my eyes filled with joyful tears, my friend looked at me with great concern and said, "Are you okay?"

I looked at her and said, "Yes, I am so overwhelmed with gratitude. What did I do to deserve to be right here"?

She looked at me and said, "It is simple; you deserve to be here because of who you are!"

I will never forget those words and will never forget what that moment meant to me.

His Holiness was remarkable, genuine and funny as ever. He said, "I am just a man, a simple man, one eyebrow up, one eyebrow down, you can join me for tea any time."

Oh my, how I would love to have tea with him. His time with us was nothing short of breathtaking, full of humor, full of humanitarian stories, facts and fun. He confirmed to me that to be happy is our birthright. Being happy is given to us by someone much bigger than us; being happy is a choice and being happy is easy because you choose it.

No one can buy happiness; no one can bargain happiness and no one other than yourself can make you feel the true happiness that comes from your soul unless you allow it. The Dalai said, "You will know when you have found your happiness."

The tears of joy continued to flow and I embraced every moment of being in his presence. I did not want this time to end.

What I leaned from the conference and the many lesson in life is, fear is a feeling and faith is a choice. For me, if I fear what is going to happen in my life, I will certainly lose sight of my faith that I will get through it.

On this day I was really boggled, and blasted with so much "yumminess" I really couldn't get a grasp on what I just experienced.

I thought about this panel for years after the experience. I came to believe that science gives us facts and faith cuts us loose from the bondage of reality. Maybe that is where so many scientists have had to take that "leap of faith" to discover so much.

So maybe, just maybe faith and science really are one in the same.

When pain and challenges of life find their way into our world, we have two choices. One, allow the pain to run your life, or run with life and find your happiness. I did!

♪♫♪

"Somebody Bigger Than You and I"
Elvis

"

Only the most naive of questions
are truly serious.

"

Milan Kundera

CHAPTER 11

BOSTON WAS A BLESSING

Value: Health

Just when we think we have a plan, He reminds us to think again. Picture this: Being one class away from a certification that you have worked for so hard, planned for the next steps and even gone out on a limb to test your courage. Believing you were ready to fly, yet life takes you by surprise and in a completely different direction. What would you do?

It has been said that if you want to make God laugh, tell him your plans. He laughs at me quite often and I am happy he does for I would not be here laughing at myself now.

There was a time when I was not laughing. I was actually crying a lot! Being a stubborn little redhead I had to realize my plan was not always the right plan. What is the right plan?

Not realizing what that question really meant to me took me straight to Boston, where I learned what it really meant. And what being so blessed means.

Working in the school, I believe they pay me to play. Truly being able to say "I love my job" only makes it easier to focus on what

I love and that is working with the youth. I feel I have found my fountain of youth as they keep me young in mind, young at heart and open to surprises every day.

One of the great perks of working in the school is having five weeks off during the summer, long weekends, and all the school breaks. This job has been very conducive to being a mommy.

This particular summer I thought I had it all planned out. I only had one more class to finish the second level of my Life Coach course. I was chosen to step into the Master Level of teaching other coaches. This opportunity was not one to take lightly. It wasn't just an opportunity, it was a crazy wild opportunity. I was selected to go to Paris and assist in a program that would take me out of my bubble and into a bigger world. I thought I was ready for it.

I studied French, worked with a mentor to teach me the culture, had my summer plans down to a "T," even my flight and housing for a month in Paris.

Then I got the news. My mom was diagnosed with cancer, a rare, aggressive carcinoma. No one in our local area knew how to remove it or even work with it. Was this really happening NOW? I know we are not supposed to ask God why, yet I did. Why and how can this happen to her again? This was not her first bout with cancer and she had already had two open heart surgeries. This woman is a trooper, a fighter and someone who I really didn't know because she was not a "talker." I never understood how I was such a talker and she wasn't. There was so much to know about her and as a child I just didn't understand why she didn't talk as much as me.

For the longest time, I thought she had given me away.

I had issues of abandonment for years and our connection was not what I always dreamed of having in a mother-daughter relationship.

I tried for years to talk with her, yet her pain of the past was too much. By not talking about the past, it left me with so much to wonder, too much to assume and not enough to believe we would have the strength to ever have the loving relationship I always hoped for.

When we got the news of her cancer, all those emotions went straight out the window. It didn't matter what happened in the past and out of my control. What mattered was being able to be with her through this and praying she could be a two-time cancer survivor.

After many doctor appointments, a lot of research looking for that one special doctor who works with this kind of cancer, the decision was made for her to go to Boston to have the surgery.

That is when my plan became God's plan. Because I was the only one in the family who had summers off, it was best for the family that I go with her. So I did.

Again I planned or so I thought I did, just how I could go to Boston and still finish my last class in my Life Coach course for this level. I thought even my flight arrangements could still stay on course for Paris. It would have been crazy, yet in theory, it could have worked.

This was the plan: Fly to Boston, get the surgery, mom flies home, I fly to San Francisco, finish my last class, take the exam and then fly to Paris. Call me crazy, yet that was my plan.

Knowing Boston was bigger than me and this surgery was bigger than all of us, I was not quite sure what I was going to do or even feel since this was going to be the first time my mother and I would be in such a vulnerable situation together.

A lot of time together, a lot of time to reflect and a lot of time to talk, which was something we did not do a lot of. Of course we talked in everyday life but not about the past, not about her wants and desires and certainly not about her feelings.

Being a deeply emotional person, I always said, "I must have been adopted because I am the mushy one in the family." I always enjoy going to that "warm fuzzy place" and love to have "deep conversations," yet I knew that was not going to happen. What could I do to help this issue and to make the best of this venture? I had it—I would call my niece, Jessica Ruth.

Grandparents are not supposed to have favorites. It is better to say "special ones" in the family, yet it was very obvious who my mother's "special one" is. This was not a bad thing, because I knew having my niece with us would make my mom happy and if that is all I could do against the odds of this cancer, then so be it.

The three of us got on an airplane scared as all get-out about what was in the realm of the unknown.

We arrived in Boston to the hotel next to the Dana-Farber Cancer Institute. We checked into our room, which at that point we did not know would be home for the next 19 days. We scoped out the neighborhood and went to dinner to make a plan.

Our first plan was to build our calendar for the next, so we thought, week or so. Put in the doctor appointments, meetings with the "team," scope out the local grocery store.

I knew in able to keep our spirits up in a time that could get very ugly, I had to be the "big girl" and make a lot of decisions while also keeping the family at home well informed.

I also knew I had to keep me, myself, and I focused on my health both emotionally and physically as well. I made a promise to myself to go out once a day to discover something. If my niece chose to join me, then I would really have to make it special as we were in the heart of Boston.

There was so much to see, so much history, and so many people.

I was used to my bubble of a quaint little home town where the speed limit on the main street is 15 miles per hour. So this big city was a place I hoped would give me life lessons while I was trying to "keep it all together."

We met with the team and I asked a lot of naive questions. We also met the main doctor, the one who was aware of this crazy cancer fight. She said, "We will see what we can do." That was not hopeful enough for me! I needed to know that this superwoman was not going to lose her cape with this battle.

I call my mom that because as an adult and watching her go through her battles she has shown me the FIGHT she has in her. The fight for life!

They told us after a series of tests her surgery would be in a week.

We then, as much as she was able, started sightseeing as tourists. We learned how to use the subway, had great dinners on the pier, visited the Boston Tea Party Ship and walked the Freedom Trail. My goodness that town opened my eyes to so much. Not just history, but to the strength my mom and I had together.

As I was studying my Life Coach course, I was simultaneously studying A Course in Miracles with a phenomenal women and mentor in Carmel, California. Nadja Giese, being a redhead with a freckled face and a strong, spirited, spunky soul, was a woman of my own heart and taught me so much!

The one main lesson came when she pointed out to me the moment when I had experienced a major turning point in my life. I remember describing to her a dream I had of being blindfolded and then taking it off.

Her response was, "You are now awake to your life." Nadja and this Course in Miracles took me to a different place of appreciation and understanding of life.

Would you believe, when I was packing for Boston I forgot and left my Course in Miracles study book at home? It had become like a security blanket. Don't get me wrong, I do have a Bible, yet I already knew He was with me every day.

I enjoyed taking this private course and being mentored by this phenomenal woman. What was I going to do without my book to keep me occupied? No Life Coach books to study and magazines where not holding my interest.

So I told my niece, "I need to find a bookstore and buy my course book." Of course a bookstore would have it, right? Wrong. No bookstore near the hospital had the book. We made several phone calls and the last person said, "If you take the subway for about half hour north, there is a little book store that might have it." She was right, they did! Guess what my niece and I did?

While my mom was resting up for the surgery, yep, my niece and I conquered the subways. We found our way to that quaint little bookstore, purchased the book, then walked out of the store to pure amazement.

Looking out the door of this beautiful little store across the street, I saw a red brick archway with a narrow path proceeding it. In my "wandering mind" I thought, "what could be on that path?" I ask my niece if she would be willing to venture with me and see. There were no signs that I could see and no "do not enter" notices posted.

So, we went. Crossing the street I remember saying to myself, "What are you doing?" "What will we find?" and "Where will it take us?"

Going through the archway I saw beautiful plants, breathtaking landscape and a quiet man making all this beauty happen.

As we strolled slowly down this narrow path I looked at my niece and said, "This is so beautiful, it is like the secret garden."

The kind man started laughing with us and then he said, "You don't know where you are, do you?"

I look at him, embarrassed that he'd heard my silly little comment. I really did not know where I was.

He replied sweetly, "You are in the garden of Harvard University."

Oh my words! I really did stumble my way to a place that was breathtaking.

In all my days of schooling, I never imagined being at Harvard. It never even entered my mind that I would ever be "good enough" for such a place. And look, here we were.

I thanked the kind gentleman for waking me up to reality and guiding us to the Harvard Library. He explained that the campus was open and for us to enjoy our "secret garden."

As we made our way through this beautiful campus we found the library. Up the stairs we went, all along my niece saying, "Auntie we cannot go in there; they might know we are not students here."

I quickly replied back, "Oh baby girl, we are students of life and we just have to own it. Act like we belong here and no one will care."

Well, someone cared because as quickly as we arrived at the top of the stairs ready to go in, a woman stopped us and said, "The library is closed unless you have a special campus pass." She didn't want to say it, but finally told us, "Due to the terrorist alerts, the library is closed."

As soon as she said those words, I knew I had to be awake and aware of all my surroundings in my "rainbow and unicorn world."

 We had snacks in our backpack so we sat on the steps of the Harvard Library for just a bit and then made our way back to the subway. Back to the hotel and back to a situation for which I was praying for a miracle.

Now having that book with me, I was able to focus on areas that Nadja helped point out. I received my inner strength knowing we all were in the greatest hands of all.

One thing I can say is, we laughed. My niece and I every night would play cards or a word game. Sometimes we would even just look out the hotel window way up high and laugh like the characters on the show Friends looking out their window. "Oh look at that person dancing over there," or "What is that cat doing on the curtain?" or "Oh my, don't look!". We did laugh a lot which made my mom laugh, and they do say laughter is the best medicine. She certainly was getting her daily dose.

The surgery was scheduled, everyone was ready, and then they set the date. It was three days before my final exam in San Francisco and my date to leave for Paris.

How can that be? Why can't they do it sooner? Many questions went through my head.

How can I get out of my head and be here where I need to be? The family was counting on me to be "the big girl." I felt I could not show any signs of being upset over anything other than what was at hand.

I had already made all my plans and life just changed it!

I found myself once again on the lawn of Harvard. It was such a beautiful place. I had to call my pillar in life. No, this time it was not my best friend. I called the person who gives life to me in a way like no other: My daughter!

> "
> **Momma, you are just where you are supposed to be.**
> "

Sitting there crying like a baby, I didn't even want her to know how upset I was over the change in plans. I held my composure and explained what was happening with the surgery. She knew my plans for Paris and she said, "Momma, you are just where you are supposed to be."

I knew that and I knew what I had to do.

That didn't make it easier or less painful.

The surgery took place and miracles did happen! They were able to remove the one-in-a-million tumor from a very difficult and delicate location.

We discovered after the surgery the doctor who removed it became the Chief of Surgery and was recognized for her specialty with this cancer. We were all blessed that my mom was back on the road to happy healing and good health.

She was happy, yet still hurting from surgery. How much longer would we need to be here before she could get on a plane and go home? Her doctor explained, "Just about a week or so."

At this point there was no possible theory that would get me to my class and final exam in San Francisco or even on that other flight to Paris.

I went to my mom, knowing she was not a talker and knowing she was out of danger, to see what she would say, if she said anything at all. I asked her, "What would you do? Would you go or would you stay?"

She looked right at me without hesitation and said, "I would go!"

My heart skipped several beats. I really did not know how to take that. And I was taken by surprise. I didn't know how to respond to that other than losing my breath. I said, "Really?" and then no other words were said. She did not explain what she meant and I didn't ask.

Again I held my composure, made sure everything was okay at the time and that my niece was feed, and then I fled! I had to take myself for a walk so no one would know how upset I really was.

After a good walk and amazing sights, I knew in my heart it does not matter what someone else would do. What mattered to me was I knew I had made the right choice for me. When it comes to health, I never take it for granted.

My mother had been through a lot with her health. How could I put her on one airplane and me on another? Besides, Pairs wasn't going anywhere and with everything I had learned, well, I just learned a lot more!

Many years later I received a card from my mom. In it, she wrote, "It was your smiles that got me through it all."

What a confirmation to smile every day, because you really do not know what a difference it makes to someone else!

My mom has been through a lot and still, she perseveres.

My mom is my silent hero.

♫ ♪

"Time"
Pink Floyd

"

*Freedom means having
nothing else to lose.*

"

Former President George W. Bush

CHAPTER 12

FINDING FREEDOM IN THE TREES

Value: Joy

With no political views, just seeing his yummy words, former President George W. Bush put it so profoundly! "When you have nothing else to lose you are free."

Free of what, you ask? What do you want to be free of? That is the question!

At the time, I was still working fulltime at the school. I was a big girl now, working at the high school and in my 25th year of coaching cheerleaders from Pop Warner to high school to now at our local community college. I knew what it took to lead a team of 26 college girls: A lot of time!

For me the value of joy kept me focused on the fun that had developed to this point. I was a happy momma with two wonderful young adults on their way to successful lives and hopefully making me a grammie one day. How happy would that make me? I truly felt if my kiddos were healthy and happy and my mom was on the mend, I could move forward and focus on the fun waiting to be had.

Little did I know what I was about to embrace.

Time passed and I knew it was time I retire my cheerleader coach pom-poms at the college level to make myself available for two grandbabies on the way. First from my daughter, then my son— both just nine months apart. I knew I was going to be busy with babies. Now that is something to cheer about!

My life went to a whole new level and I knew I was ready for "grammie glory." Little did I know what other gift was waiting to guide me.

I owe this change and gentle guidance to the next fabulous fork in the road, to an incredible soul named John Mims.

I thought, "When would I have any more time in my life to meet another commitment other than grand babies?" I responded several times to him when he asked, "What do you think about Rotary?" I would say, "Let me get back to you." Being the patient man he is, he waited.

Then I told myself, I spent a lot of time with the cheerleaders and having all that time free now, maybe I do have time for grand babies and this place called Rotary!

After two years of patience, now a newbie to Rotary, thank you John Mims for changing my path in life.

He will never know just how grateful I am for his patience in helping me discover my heart's desire.

For two years he would say in his gentle way, "There is this organization I think you would love. You don't have to do anything but be you."

In my naive world, I really did not know what that statement meant at the time. Yet I trusted him and knew he would not get me into something he was not in himself. Rotary rescued my spirit.

I did not talk a lot in the meetings. I was like a deer in headlights each week, just in awe of what was being presented. I felt so honored to be in a room with such incredible community leaders.

There was another new member who joined right before me. I owe so much appreciation to Frank Giglio for opening a door of joy I could not have dreamed of.

Frank had just completed his time in Nicaragua in the Peace Corps and landed in our club. Being a new chapter of Rotary, the members were still making their way in developing and discovering who they were and what direction to go as a community/global club. Even though I was new and still not quite certain what my place was in this new found "yumminess," I knew I wanted to be a part of these incredible people.

I remember clear as day; Frank raised his hand and said, "Do you have an international project?"

Everyone, as if it were planned, simultaneously said, "NO!" He then explained how he just finished his time in Nicaragua. He talked about what he did there and mentioned Los Quinchos Orphanage. He explained he was going back to Nicaragua in two weeks. Was there anyone who wanted to join him for an assessment trip? The club was all about that!

John Mims raised his hand to volunteer. Off they went and two weeks later they presented a slide show to the club. Frank then said, "I am going again." Before he could finish the words, "Who wants to go?", my hand was up!

One other member raised his hand. Oh my words, what did I do? I had never been out of the country and I did not have a clue as to what to do next.

I did know I was making the trip with three men and felt I had nothing to worry about.

All the arrangements were made and we were off. Frank, John Mims, Terry and me. I was the only girl and I didn't think twice since I was raised in a family that was all boys except for me. One thing I had to keep in mind was I could not "be a girl" and cry. I felt I had to be tough like the guys, even if I got scared.

Nicaragua is one of the poorest countries in the world, which became obvious the moment we arrived. I saw things as I got off the airplane that I could never have imagined. What had I gotten myself into?

Frank's Peace Corps group had already left, so his connections in the country included a Rotarian name Dr. Ricardo, the founder of the orphanage he worked at, and a few friends. He quickly contacted Dr. Ricardo to let him know we had arrived in the country.

Not sure just what the plan was, Frank took us to the orphanage. His team had installed the first latrine at the girls' site known as the Youska the previous year.

Among the children's major needs was shoes. Our next thought was, "Let's go get shoes, 79 pairs of them." I will never forget what it felt like to buy 79 pairs of shoes all at one time!

The market in Nicaragua is one of the largest in Central America. We found our way to the "shoe boutique" that had a wall of black leather shoes and so much more in every inch of a very small location.

One of the directors of the Youska went with us to buy the shoes. It never entered my mind how she was going to "fit" the children to the particular shoe size until she brilliantly popped out her "paper drawn, measured foot" of each child with the child's name on each drawing! How brilliant was that?

Frank helped with the language barrier. The store manager and the Youska's director all measured each one of those shoes. When we entered the boutique there was an ocean of black on the walls; by the time we left there where many holes to fill. We not only made a difference in the lives of all those children receiving the shoes, we also made a difference in the lives of those who sold us the shoes!

As I was sitting in the boutique I looked up and saw a red metallic cherub in a heart hanging from the doorway. I looked at Terry and asked, "What is today's date?"

He said, "February 14." Oh my words, it was Valentine's day!

I am not real big on Valentine's Day, no pun intended. I instantly thought, "I am in a shoe store buying 79 pairs of shoes, none of them for me. I am with three perfect gentlemen, none of them are mine. I am doing something so much bigger than me, how can that be? What a perfect Valentine's gift to all"

My heart warmed with that thought. Valentine's Day would never be the same. It would absolutely be better!

After so many amazing connections and experiences, we came to our final day before leaving Nicaragua. What at first had seemed to be an ugly place had turned out to be more beautiful than I ever imagined. The place needed help, yet the people, oh my words, the people—pure and simple, just beautiful!

Frank felt we had not experienced the peak of the beauty in this country until we had zip-lined. What? As in tall trees? What? No way! Yet I remembered my original pledge not to act like a girl and to be tough like the guys. I thought, "Can I do this? Am I strong enough to face that fear? Will I let the guys down?"

The first ramp at the zip-line park was high in the air and had a carving on it that read, "Hakuna matata," which means "no worries." Wrong! I was worried. I had never done anything so adventurous, I knew I had to TRY. I knew I had to face this fear!

With John Mims going down the zip-line before me, I saw that he was okay. The guide put the latch on my harness, put my hands on the line and said, "Now go." Again he said, "Now go." One more time he said, "NOW GO."

I could not go! I was frozen!

I heard Terry behind me say, "Let her be, she will go when she can." Oh my words, he had my back and I knew at that moment it was not about going. For me, it was about letting go.

I stood there in those trees high above land thinking of my life as it was. Where I had come from and where I was going. At that moment I looked at the ground, then looked at the sky and said as my phenomenal niece Lindsey always said, "Hakuna Matata." Then I said to the Lord, "If this is my day to die, dear Lord, I thank you for my life and this is a good day to die, amen." AND I LET GO!

OH MY WORDS! The most invigorating and exhilarating experience of my life.

I believe, as I have said, "from the mouths of babes we learn great lessons" and the lessons I learned and the love I received from this baby we called Lindsey showed me life, showed me smiles, and reminds me every day, "Hakuna Matata." Even in the trees of Nicaragua.

Fourteen trees and a million smiles later I touched the ground. Now the words of George Addair, "Everything you have ever wanted is on the other side of fear," mean so much more to me.

> **Everything you have ever wanted is on the other side of Fear.**
>
> – George Addair

What I have discovered is that fear is an emotion, not a condition. And there is nothing to fear but fear itself. Letting go at the top of those trees helped me to let go of so many fears.

Fear of failing, fear of unknown conditions, fear of love, and fear of growing up. Fear of not knowing what's next just flew away in those trees.

Time to let go and move forward, as I found freedom and fun in a situation that some would say is crazy.

Before leaving Nicaragua, Frank wanted to take us back to Los Quinchos to bid farewell and see if the orphanage would be willing to work with us in the future.

Of course they were, and the connections made at that point were priceless.

As we were leaving the site, I felt myself start to tear up. I told myself, "Don't be a girl, don't cry." As I was holding it in with all my might, Frank said, "It's okay to cry." That's all it took.

I cried like a baby. Cried for the people, cried for feeling like we did not do enough, cried because I was so grateful for the doors that were opened. Now my view of "being a girl" took on an entirely new meaning for me. Being a girl, discovering my strengths, taking that "leap of faith," guided me to where I am today.

Now I ask myself, "What is next?" and "When?" Now is the time. For what, I didn't have a clue. I just kept feeling IT. Was that IT my "volcano of SKITTLES" ready to erupt? My colorful rainbow of sweetness for life! Time will tell. All I knew at this point was the question I kept asking myself, "Don't ask why now, ask why not now?"

Just put one foot in front of the other and see what is next. You can do it!

"Hakuna Matata"
Lion King Sound Track

"

*Life happens when you are
making other plans.*

"

John Lennon

CHAPTER 13

CUTTING THE APRON STRINGS

Value: Family

My only goal in life at one time was to be a mommy. While I was planning life, life had more plans for me. Now my two are young adults planning their own lives.

Feeling very blessed to have a home with a white picket fence and the lemon tree in the backyard while they were growing up gave me hope for the future. Facing the fact that my husband and I were growing apart and it was affecting the family far too often, showing its ugly face, made me rethink the future.

It really was a home with a lot of love, a lot of entertainment and a lot of family. That is what got me through the storms.

They say, "Home is where the heart is," and my heart, at the best of its ability, certainly was making our home as happy and healthy as possible.

My son put it so sincerely, so simply, and as sensibly as he could when he told me he was ready to move out and start his life. My eyes teared up, as I was not sure I had given him all the tools of life he needed.

He looked at me and said, "You did, Mom. All you need to do now is cut the apron string. Just cut it. Go ahead, you can. It will be okay."

At that moment I knew he was ready. I knew as I was planning life, life was planning something more. My daughter, being headstrong and ready for life, had already moved out and I knew she was ready for the world. The question was, is the world ready for her?

She was born almost two months premature. The doctors told us she might not make it to her first birthday. Something inside me said, "No way, she is here for a reason," and I was not letting her go. Family got us through that time even though no one could visit till she was two months old.

The larger family has always been a focus for fun. Extended family adds even more fun. And my two best accomplishments in life tops it all! Family has been strong even through the storms. That is when my "rainbow and unicorns" show up and shut down the challenge at hand. I was not truly ready for either of my children to move out and move on with their lives. They were both ready and I knew I had to get ready for what life has planned for me.

I would not wish divorce on my worst enemy. Since it was my choice, it was also my choice to fight for a fun future.

Some people say you are not family if you are not blood-related. I am here to tell you the definition of family in my book reads like this: Family: faith, fun, and friends are family all bundled into one, and always gives strength, power, love, and life.

I have discovered when times are tough family is tougher and it is not always about blood connection. When planning life after a hurricane, I saw it in the eyes of so many who lost their jobs, lost their homes and for many, lost their hope.

After my children found their paths to adulthood, I found my path and hope in a place called Rotary! My Rotary family rescued my spirit and gave me hope for happiness after I had accomplished my goal of parenting the children to the best of my abilities.

I am a proud member of The Rotary Club of Monterey Pacific, in District 5230.

This joyful place opened my eyes, my heart and my soul to something so much bigger than me. That is not too hard to top since I am under five feet tall!

However, Rotary is bigger than me and it allowed me to get bigger in my life and in the world.

The doors that have opened, I could never have dreamed of in a million years. Family support as I have walked through those doors is more than I could ever ask for.

My son doesn't always say it, yet I do believe he is happy to see me doing good for others. He may not pick up trash with us, yet he will give the shirt off his back to anyone in need and doesn't blink an eye! He does it with heart and soul and that is what

makes a true Rotarian. Having a heart for others. Service Above Self. Giving of yourself with no expectations in return. This is the perfect picture of my son!

My daughter is right there as well, and both my children are always brainstorming for opportunities.

Giving to others without expectations in return has special meaning for a family that cannot expand beyond man and wife, cannot give birth, and feels incomplete without a child. This is a family that has taken on a whole new meaning...

Giving the ultimate gift to the meaning of family was just what my daughter did years after she witnessed and supported me in Rotary.

Her gift was not done in the world of Rotary, yet I did gift her with a Rotary high honor, a Paul Harris Award, for giving such a gift to the world. She and her brother always reward me with the honor of being their momma.

She made someone else a momma. She did not do this for any award or for any other reason than just to give life to someone who could not. Actually, she did it twice.

Some people give blood, some people give an organ. My Princess gave life. She was a surrogate mom, twice. "Baby Friend" (nickname) was born first and she was the topic of many conversations with the first question being, "How can she give a baby away?" She did not "give a baby away," she was the angel oven that baked the seeds of two other loving people who can now extend their family. "Baby Friend" lives in Los Angeles with her family.

We all then got ready for round two, two years later with the second surrogate, "Pumpkin" (nickname) who is a child of China born in the month of October. Talk about amazing.

To see that child come out of the body of my baby, life will never be the same. It will be better. Connecting the two countries through the breath of life, well, no need to say more!

I could not be more honored to be the momma of two incredible souls who really put the "m" in family. "M" as in magic, the magic of love and everything it means to us!

Magic happens in the moments that gives someone life, and they do give me life. That is the gift that keeps on giving.

When it comes to gifts that keep on giving, I gave one that I didn't know the value of until the day it was received.

I met a woman named Reva who was celebrating her 100th birthday. I was blessed to happen into her path of life and family.

I was helping my cousin serve the early morning meal at her bed and breakfast inn to a dining room filled with one family in town to celebrate, with the town, their mother's 100th birthday. Reva was like the mom of an entire town and they all considered themselves family.

As I spoke with one of her sons, he shared with us all the good his mother did in town over the years. This included writing two books and working on a third.

The first book was about the trains of Dunsmuir, and the second was about the secret recipes of life. When I found out she was working on a third book, I knew I wanted to meet her and find out just what her secret to life was!

I ask her son if she would be willing or able to meet with me briefly before their celebration in the city park. He did not know if she would be resting or had other plans before the fun waiting for her by the entire town. Could you imagine having an entire town celebrate your life while you are still living? Talk about living life!

I told the son I totally understood if my last minute request could not be met. I was honored to meet the family of a woman who had given so much to her community and will continue to give with her books and stories from all those who were blessed to know her.

After breakfast and clean up at the inn, my cousin and I went for a wonderful walk in the quaint, beautiful little community known as Dunsmuir. We were at least three blocks from the inn when that same gentleman I spoke with at breakfast approached us, breathing hard from running to find us saying, "She will see you."

I said joyfully and loudly, "What, when?"

In a split second and in his overly excited voice, he said "Now!"

I was honored that he took the time to see if it could happen and even more honored that he looked for me and was ready to take us to her.

I was overwhelmed with gratitude that she would actually give me time on her busy and special day.

We walked into her sweet little well-decorated living room with knickknacks that she must have been collecting all her life. She was 100 years young that day!

Just looking at the knickknacks kept my cousin and me entertained until this stunning tall woman came out of the kitchen, using her walker. Her silver hair was all done up, and she wore red lipstick and a beautiful long dress. What an amazing gift to be in the company of someone so alive and so present.

She began the conversation by thanking us for wanting to see her. Can you believe that? Within seconds I knew just why this community loved her so. In no rush at all, we had a joyful conversation. She told us how honored she was to have so many people love her, how her entire town was like her family.

She told us about her knickknacks, about the trains, showed us her books and signed them so we would remember her. As if I could ever forget her!

I recall telling her of my work with the youth and told her I loved her perspective on life.

I asked her, "If you could share something—words, guidance, tips, or a secret to life—that I could take back home and share with the youth, what would it be?"

I will never forget it. She looked at me with tears in her eyes! I said, "Oh my, I am sorry if I said anything …"

"No, no," she replied.

She then looked at me with the most beautiful sparkle in her eyes. She sat up very tall on the sofa and said, "You have given me the greatest gift of all today. You passing on my words to the youth is something I could never have imagined getting today."

She continued "Well, let me tell you. There are three secrets to life. The first is to have a long term goal. Something to aspire to. The second is to have a short term goal. Something to accomplish soon. And the third, well, the third is to take a lot of naps!"

That was her secrets to a long and beautiful life.

We all started laughing and embraced with joyful hugs. She walked us to the door and with a gleam in her eye, she said thank you to us.

How can I ever give thanks enough to such an incredible soul? Sharing her words, keeping her visit in my heart and remembering that magical moment in time will certainly be one of my secrets to what I hope will be a long healthy and happy life.

After the visit in this quaint and joyful little town, spending fun times with my cousin, who has since passed, life definitely had a plan for me but I could not see it. Yet I could certainly feel it. I remember saying. "I feel something big is going to happen. I just don't know what it is, but I can feel it!"

♪ ♫ ♪

"Blessed"
Martina McBride

"

Too much of a good thing can be wonderful.

"

May West

CHAPTER 14

ANITA

Value: Happiness

Anita was four years old, big brown eyes, a smile to melt your heart and tiny dirty little feet. The minute I saw her for the second time, she remembered me!

She was three years old last year when we first entered the dumps in Managua, Nicaragua. For the second time with our Rotary International project, with me teaching the youth as part of a "culture experience," I led a team of eight cherubs (students) and four adults into another life-changing experience.

Taking food, crafts, toys and our presence into the center of Los basureros (the dumps) opened the eyes of my students like no classroom experience could ever offer.

Once Anita recognized me from the year prior, she decided she wanted to play peek-a-boo.

She ran around the center for a few laps, then I saw her step through the gates of the center into the big world of the dumps! I knew many people lived in the dumps of Managua, Nicaragua. I just did not realize how many!

Part of my first training for this area was the instruction: Do not leave the center. DO NOT go into the dumps without guidance.

All that went out the window when I saw Anita coaxing me on to follow her ... out the gates!

She moved much faster than I thought she could. I exited the gates and walked for a couple of moments searching for Anita. I could not see her anywhere. I looked around and realized, oh my words, we are not in Kansas anymore, Toto. There was no sign of Anita.

I started calling her name. I knew at that moment I had broken all the rules of this trip by not telling someone where I was going and by leaving the center in general without a buddy. Yet, at that moment Anita was my buddy!

It seemed like a lifetime, but it was probably more like three minutes of not knowing where I was. I kept calling for Anita and of course she was hiding from me. I felt a little hand grab my hand. It wasn't Anita, it was a little boy, maybe five or six years old. He kept saying "Anita" and pulled me deeper into the dumps. I discovered that day that over 3,000 people live in the dumps and Anita was born there.

Still walking in a direction unknown to me yet trusting the little boy was taking me right where I was supposed to be.

Before I knew it, the little boy led me into a makeshift structure with a door and a roof. Trust, that is what led me to that moment that day.

I had not a thought in the world other than finding Anita. Once in the structure, the little boy ran ahead of me, giggling as if to say, "Find me, too."

For a moment I stopped in my tracks, looked around and thought, "Oh my words, this is their front room." Exploring even more, I found a "bedroom." Walking even further into this structure I realized it had dirt floors. I thought to myself, "OH MY WORDS, this is someone's HOME all put together with items from the dumps."

Once I caught my breath I continued walking straight ahead to discover music to my ears, a lot of giggles. I saw a rusty box bed spring with yellow foam from the 1970s on top. I heard giggling from underneath it, so of course I looked! There he was, the little boy who had led me there. As I giggled back, I heard additional giggles, those of a little girl. It was Anita! I looked on top of the rusted box springs, under the yellow foam and saw tiny toes that led me to a moment I will treasure forever.

I tickled her toes and moved the foam off her. She let out the most precious yell of delight as if to say, "You found me." Her continued giggles warmed my soul and at that moment I discovered what true happiness is.

I discovered it does not matter what kind of home you live in. It doesn't matter where you live! It matters who you are with and how they make you feel, and how your heart and soul feels in the presence of those you are with.

In that moment I knew, even though I had broken all the rules of the dumps, I was right where I was supposed to be with the right person in this great big world.

All kinds of thoughts went through my mind. The most unforgettable one being, "I have reached the depth of the earth yet the joy in my heart at this moment could only be heaven-sent."

I believe angels are sent to us every day. Anita was more than an angel, she was a teacher at so many levels. I thought for a moment, "What more can I do for this baby?" She had made me so incredibly grateful for the time together, the laughter, "belly giggles," and the heart-melting smiles shared. I said to myself, "How can I give to her that level of joy?" As I was walking back to the center, it occurred to me that we brought toys and baby dolls to share with all the children. Being a cheerleader in high school and college and a cheer coach for 25 years, I was absolutely in heaven at that moment remembering there was a talking cheerleader doll in our bag of goodies.

I returned to the center, retrieved the doll and went back to Anita's home – breaking all the rules of the trip. I explained to my "cherubs" before returning to Anita's home, "If no harm is done and no laws broken, sometimes we have to break the rules to receive a priceless experience." They knew I was up to something and I took a buddy this time, my nephew Marc.

Arriving back at Anita's home, I was blessed to meet her mommy. We exchanged no words, as I didn't speak Spanish and she didn't speak English. Body language said it all. We asked if we could give Anita the doll. Mom said yes with Anita peeking from behind her. I showed Anita the doll and pulled the talking string—"YAHOO, RAH RAH ROO, CHEERS TO YOU!" Anita giggled from her belly and pulled the string again and again and again!

I could not have dreamed of taking cheerleading to the depths of the earth and for the cheers to reach beyond the glory of heaven!

We shared more hugs and smiles and with that, left the dumps. Not long after this visit, the government closed the dumps to "outsiders." I never saw Anita again. I can only hope and pray she is receiving all she needs in life as she certainly gives life to all those who are lucky enough to be around her!

♪ ♫ ♪

"You Raise Me Up"
Josh Groban

"

We've been prepared for this,
or we would not be facing this.

"

Me

CHAPTER 15

IN MY DREAM

Value: Passion

Each year I am asked, "How was your trip to Nicaragua?" Each year I reply, "Phenomenal." I always ask myself, "How can it get better than this?" And it does! I continue to say, "I could not have dreamed this if I tried."

The students, the projects, the people. The energy, the entire trip, is always more than I could ever expect.

This year opened my eyes to so much more.

Preparations for this trip certainly dealt me a hand. Planning for a team of 10 to leave the country raised the bar with far more demands. Now I certainly welcome a challenge, yet this one, being the biggest team yet, made me really get my act together with no room for failure.

Talk about a lot of self-pressure. I had to protect myself from me. I had to keep reminding myself, "It will all be okay."

I became the leader as Frank was moving to Texas. I recall him saying to me, "This is your baby now, if you choose." I am not one to turn my back on a baby, so needless to say, I so chose.

Who was I to show any fear if I was leading this team so ready to follow? I knew we were ready, except for one member. Her father kept asking, "How can you guarantee it will all be okay?"

I looked at him and had to say, "I can't." I looked at her and added, "Once we arrive there—we will not be in Kansas, Toto."

To continue, I said to her dad, "I am not God in the slightest way. I cannot make such guarantees. Yet I can guarantee you this: I will care for all these cherubs as if I gave birth to them myself."

He knew then what I said was true and I was going to hold the greatest space for each one of these cherubs. I was honored their parents trusted me with their precious bundles of joy.

Living in a community otherwise known as a bubble, a protective bubble that so many found comfort in, and going to a place in such despair was certainly a challenge. Yet each bundle of joy was ready for what was next in our plans.

Now we had 25 weeks of preparing for a cultural experience, learning how to raise funds for their travels and for our planned projects. Learning how and what is meant when I say, "You will discover the gift of receiving as you give." At first they did not know what that meant till the day came when they felt that exact emotion while little ones in San Marcos, Nicaragua, embraced them with pure love and gratitude for our precious presence.

As we were sitting in a village, one of my girls looked at me with her eyes full of tears. I heard her whisper, "I get it." Then she said, "I know now, Ms. G., why you keep coming back here." She continued, "I get it now. What more can we do?"

Those are the monumental, magical moments that take my breath away. That was the moment that confirmed all my time and effort, stress and sweat, in making these trips possible is worth every moment.

The one important requirement of this program is parent participation. Yes, a parent must be engaged and invested at this time of their child's life as I explain, "Your child will not come back the same. They will be changed little souls and I will gladly take the blame."

We raised the funds and gathered donations of sport equipment and so much more. We were planning our projects as we learned from afar what they needed. What our hosts in Nicaragua had planned for us was nothing short of giving us the stars.

They set up gatherings that made us feel like royalty. Water is scarce, food quite often is even scarcer. They set a table on the top of the courtyard overlooking the area where they were going to perform for us. The table held bottled water, fresh fruit from the surrounding trees, and a homemade porridge of which I am not quite sure of the ingredients. This all was a gift of gratitude from them as I know some of those children waiting to perform for us probably did not eat breakfast that morning. We did not need nor expected such display. We really only wanted to give from our souls and simply play.

It is one thing to know the word "gratitude." This experience helped all of us to see and FEEL what gratitude really means.

So much to see in the markets: many people, many items. With trash on the ground and many young children in the streets, it was hard to focus on American's way of shopping. Purchasing the items and stuffing backpacks too, 350 with a year's worth of school supplies. Planning a day of play was so much fun. What do we do when there is so much need? We take one step at a time and say what will be, will be.

Each day I had planned out and still there was so much need. The language barrier was too much for me.

As I booked our van with a local family, I asked if he knew of a translator who would be willing to work with a group of very active teens and a grandma too. We were blessed with his son-in-law, Denis.

This year we took an elder of our community who just wanted to share her gifts and her experience. I ask if she was prepared and she replied, "I've already packed all my gear." I would not let just anyone come along so late in the game; we are talking a week before we took off.

She assured me she had already traveled to Leon, Nicaragua. I felt her wisdom would be a great addition, and hoped she realized much time had passed and conditions had changed from the last time she had traveled to Nicaragua. Yet that did not matter. She just wanted to join us.

Wisdom of any sort is a gift. For me, wisdom and worthiness keeps showing its face regardless of all the angels who kept popping into place. The guidance I received every step of the way confirmed I was worthy no matter what my gremlins would say: Worthy of the opportunities, worthy of all the great words and worthy of the compliments that came my way.

I blush when I hear, "DiAnna you are amazing." I respond with a humbled heart. I truly feel and say, "Oh, no, I am just DiAnna, doing what I love."

Wisdom from others is always a gift. Who believes it only comes with age and experience? Part of that is true; however, I do believe wisdom is part of the soul. That is why tots to elders will always be a part of something we treasure deep in our hearts. Together Achieving Successful Kindness that is a program made for me and you.

The grandma who joined us did just that. She shared many stories and walked slowly too, which gave us all time to slow down and see our surroundings, and not just walk by all that matters and get caught up in despair.

We saw beautiful flowers and precious pets, too. The lakes and the parks gave us such a beautiful view. With so many colors, how could anyone be in despair? The people alone gave us such hope. Their happiness alone was richer than our own.

Nicaragua is known as "The land of lakes and volcanoes." Experiencing both certainly opened our eyes to a world so big!

After a full day of delivering backpacks with still more to share, I took our team to the top of a volcano. Yes, an actual active volcano that was so full of life yet in no way were we worried it would take our lives. It was totally safe for us to be up there as the tour guide kept us in a safe place.

Driving to the top of that volcano had more symbolism than I thought.

Just get to the top and you will see more than you expected—that was exactly the lesson waiting for me.

The tour guide parked the van and told us to put on the hard hats. This instruction gave us the feeling of, "What are we doing here?" The tour guide said, "You have nothing to fear. It is simply a safety act." As we strolled around we could smell the strong scent of sulfur and see the bright light in the center of the volcano. It gave us all such delight to see something so enormous and so full of life.

A volcano is a strong symbol of life, always bubbling and roaring inside. Never knowing when it will erupt, only hoping when it does, those in its path will be protected and safe.

Knowing we were safe at this time, we found ourselves looking down into a hole so enormous in size. What would we do if it started to erupt? Again the tour guide assured us we were safe.

Soon we found ourselves strolling to even at higher land, to a cross planted at the top of some rocks. Someone had built and erected a cross that could be seen from far away. From mountain to mountain you could view this cross. A cross of hope for all to see.

We should never pity anyone who has such pride as the person who built that cross! What we learned on this trip was certainly more powerful than the depths of a volcano.

The next day we still had so much to do.

In the village in Jinotepe, I discovered a place that would wake me up in a way I never imagined.

We arrived at the Church of Guadalupe to deliver art supplies. I recall so clearly as if it were yesterday. All the cherubs had gotten out of the van. I was so slow and in my own zone. I remember Denis, our translator, waiting from behind, saying to me, "We really must go." Still not looking up from the ground, I do believe I found my path to my purpose. I soon looked up and said, "Oh my!" What did I find? It was a sight so profound, it humbled my mind and stopped my heart!

Looking up from afar I saw in the distance what they call the Church of Guadalupe. I saw a cement foundation with metal pillars, no walls, a tin roof and a tall steeple.

My eyes began to fill up with tears as the only words I could find were, "I have seen this in my dreams!" The closer I got, the stronger the feeling. The power inside was more than I could handle. My tears began to pour as I knew I had been here before!

Denis ask if I was okay. All I could say was, "I have seen this place in my dreams."

Even with the language barrier, he understood what I meant.

At the end of the day, I called my daughter. I ask her, "How could this be?"

She replied, "You are in the right place at the right time doing exactly what you are supposed to be doing." She continued, "Momma, you are living your purpose!"

How did a woman of her young age become so wise and full of wisdom?

I have certainly discovered, I am living my passion and purpose!

♫♪♪

"We Are The World"
Michael Jackson

"

Speak with honesty, think with sincerity, and act with integrity.

"

Anonymous

CHAPTER 16

NO ROOM AT THE INN

Value: Honesty

When making plans that involve two countries, you must trust and be honest in all of your needs, not just what you believe you need. You must make a great plan and get all your ducks in a row, because once you leave your home country there is nowhere to go but to a place you trust and hope it will all work out.

I thought for sure since I had done outreach work in Nicaragua for years, I had all my ducks in a row.

I believed a man in Nicaragua named Carlos had my back and I would not have to worry about making any more plans. Everything was set and we were on our way. A team of eight knew what we were setting off to do. Or so we thought.

In the past we had always stayed in a place we called the "condos." It was actually the guest house that the Russians built for an Italian woman known as Zalinda, the founder and director of our beloved orphanage, Los Quinchos that we had adopted.

We showed up in San Marcos at the condos at 5 p.m., we were given such a surprise to see they were not ready for us. Not only were they not ready, they had no idea we were coming till they heard the scuttlebutt in town that the Americans had arrived.

Of course, they all hugged us and wanted us to stay, yet we quickly discovered there was no room at the inn.

They explained to us that things had changed and instead of eight beds there were now only four. Zalinda continued, "Carlos no longer works here. He has a different plan he has a problem with alcohol and he never told us you were coming!"

My heart stopped for a long moment, then I said to myself, "What would John Mims do?" I did the DiAnna shuffle as I thought of a possible plan B.

We were not in Hollywood and there were no Hyatts nearby. It was getting darker and I had a team that was tired and hungry. If you've ever worked with teenagers you know you want to always make sure they are never hungry. Just when you thought you had a team of angels, their attitudes change and you actually have a team of not-so-nice teens! Not that any of my cherubs ever got to that point; I just knew I had to do something fast!

Denis, being new to our team, just two years of experience, whispered quietly, "I have an idea if you let me explore." He continued, "I think there is a hostel right down the road."

My mind was spinning as I knew I did not have a lot of time. When it gets dark in Nicaragua, you really should be indoors at your hotel or other accommodations. Not just because it may not be safe outdoors, but also because there are no lights on the streets. I knew we had to move fast.

While in the popular tourist town of Granada in years past, I visited a hostel known to the locals as "The Hostel." The hostel was not a place I would ever choose to stay on my own — much less with a group of hormonal teenage boys and girls. It consisted of a single wide-open room with no privacy for anyone and one bathroom for 30 people. We were prepared for humble accommodations, but we weren't quite prepared for "The Hostel."

When Denis said "hostel," the word brought my mind back to Granada, and I could feel my heart beat a little faster. I would only hope, at this point, that this little village with not so many tourists would have a hostel more inviting than the one in Granada.

With that, I knew and I believed he was speaking the truth. We re-packed our bags back into the van. With hugs to our friends, we assured them we would be back the following day.

Minutes away, this great place appeared. Guess what the name was of a hostel so near?

Casa del Angel was waiting for us!

With the language barrier being so big and clear, Denis went to work doing what he did best: keeping me calm and informed.

He met with the registration desk

manager and quickly discovered they had enough rooms for us. Thank you Jesus for bringing us to a place I now call my second home. Now they tell me once they know I am coming, "Your bedroom is ready, welcome home."

This wonderful little hostel is sweeter than syrup. It has 10 bedrooms and a kitchen too. To top it off, it also has a coffee café! The beautiful garden in the center court welcomes many conversations under the stars.

A welcoming lobby has hosted great moments, as we have had meetings there in which we made delicate decisions that have changed the world.

Denis was our hero as he took my fears far way and we started the week with a whole bunch of play. He is so humble and has great pride. He is a man of his word and a hard worker too. He is the best translator and friend a team could ever ask for. What would we do without this incrediable soul we call Denis!

Denis Antonio Ruiz Menza

· · ·

Honesty is important in life. With it comes trust, with that comes openness, with that comes opportunity and with that comes priceless experiences!

♫♪♩

"Somewhere Over the Rainbow"
Israel "IZ" Kamakawiwo'ole

"

*Being happy doesn't mean that everything
is perfect. It means that you've decided
to look beyond the imperfections.*

"

Gerard Way

CHAPTER 17

UNIVERSAL LANGUAGE

Value: Trust

They say the greatest gifts in life are free. I do believe that is so. We cannot buy happiness, we cannot buy love, and we certainly cannot buy all those beautiful sights in the sky. Rainbows are a promise that it will all be okay!

Trust is a value that is kind of like the air we breathe. You cannot see it; you can only believe it is there and once you release any fear, you can certainly trust whatever is there. Trust in the language you cannot speak, trust in the language that is meant to be.

There are so many languages in this world and the greatest one has no words.

The language of love, the language of music and the language of a simple smile are all universal languages that are found throughout the world!

I recall the first time I visited Los Quinchos orphanage in San Marcos, Nicaragua. It was all about having no words. I had to rely on my body language skills, using my hands and facial expressions. Confusing yet joyful expressions to say the least!

Many of the girls came lovingly up on us, wanting to know all they could learn about the Americans who came to visit them.

A full day of play was beyond intense, the connections made without a word. Who needs words when you have such powerful smiles? That sweet little girl came to me, putting her finger on a Rotary hat pin I was wearing that said, "Make Dreams Real." She pointed with a questioning look without having the words to ask. I repeated slowly, one word at a time, "Make ... dreams ... real" She repeated the best she could. Without confidence, she said it so clearly, "Make ... dreams ... real" I hugged her so dearly and then she took me for a stroll, Showing me everything of her home sweet home.

Of course, all 39 girls wanted my attention, so one by one I gave them a hug. Talk about feeding your soul. All it took was one little look into the eyes of those girls who needed so much to learn a hug is just a hug till it is received with love!

It wasn't long before that same little girl who stood taller than me pointed at her cheek as she said in English, "I ... want ... a ... kiss"

I was totally clueless and thought she was attempting to teach Spanish to me. So I repeated, "I ... want ... a ... kiss" I repeated the phrase again and again. Then the lights came on! "I want a kiss!" Holy moly, how sweet is this?

I gave her a kiss and in return she gave me the biggest hug I could have ever earned simply by giving her a moment of my time.

Speaking of earning, I did just that. Over a bit of time, I earned enough vacation time that immersed me to the language of love in Paris! Nope, not with a lover, yet with the best group of love bugs. I went as a chaperon with the Spanish and French club from school.

Twenty-nine students, three adults and I was not the leader. Boy, did I have to hold my words not once, not twice, yet several times as the tour guide had no sense of time. Rush, rush, rush was his plan. Yet, boy, did we see a lot without any downtime. We spent nine days traveling between Paris and Spain. What an experience I joyfully sustained. From the Eiffel Tower to Notre Dame. Did you know there are 20,000 lights on the Eiffel Tower? Notre Dame had such a high tower, the entire time we were there I thought, "Where is my prince to rescue me from this wonderful tower?"

We walked every day and discovered so much!

Being a chaperon I herded the cats from the back of the line of a whole bunch of very active cherubs! After a while the students began to notice I was taking a lot of pictures of doors.

After a few hundred pictures and calling out loud, "Just one more, this is an incredible door," one of the cherubs came up to me and said, "Why, Ms. Gamecho, are you taking so many pictures of doors?"

I quickly responded, "Can you imagine who walked through these doors? Hundreds of years and hundreds of special souls. Does your mind ever wonder how much longer will these doors continue to open and close?"

I continued to explain, "Some of these doors are older than our own country—what could be more beautiful than that one special door?" It wasn't long before I realized the cherubs were coming to me without any words, just pointing and insinuating, "Take a picture of that door!"

I found myself looking back to the time when I thought my world had crashed, back in Boston where I had to make a choice, knowing Paris wasn't going anywhere.

Now I was here in Paris doing far more than I would have then! I kept telling myself I would have never experienced Paris the way I did now had I made the trip back then. I call this trip the craziest, wildest, most insane fun I have ever had. Why? Well, let me tell you. We had 29 students and three adults, and the tour program put us together with another school with 30 more students, four adults and still just ONE tour guide. He sure was herding cats like crazy!

I had to trust this tour guide in every sense of the word, me not being the leader and learning how to be a "good follower." I did just that with very few words. That is a challenge in itself since I am always talking and asking questions. On this trip I wanted to trust and travel and let the adults lead by example so I could embrace as much as possible.

Not a single word was said as we walked the beach of Normandy and quietly visited the cemetery. Being there in person was a lesson and experience you can never receive from a book at school. It gave us all a whole new meaning of D-day.

Riding from Paris to Spain on the Fast Train was an experience in itself. I arrived in Spain without being able to speak the language fluently. Guess what I did instead?

Smiling a lot and winking an eye, I certainly was able to put on a good disguise. Of course I was able to speak a little bit, yet what I needed still had not yet presented itself.

Just when I thought it couldn't get any better, I found myself at the top of a prayer rock in Barcelona where I felt closest to heaven my heart could imagine.

With my head close to the clouds and my feet on solid ground, there are very few words to express all those feelings. As I reached deep in my soul, I held the words to my heart: "Thank you for all this universal healing."

From the depths of the earth in the dumps of Nicaragua to the peak of the hills in Barcelona, I felt closest to heaven. I believe it is real, right here on earth. I felt it in both places as my heart was filled with the universal language of love.

The magic continued when I returned home, as our Rotary year was coming to an end. I will never forget one board meeting. Blame it on the wine I was drinking while taking notes. Our club meets at 5:15 p.m.—some call us the "drinking club," yet I prefer to say, "We are the happy club that meets at the happy hour." I remember listening to the board meeting without saying any words, just learning and deciding how to do more.

At the end of the meeting the president asked if there was any more business. I don't know why I did, but I did it. I raised my hand and asked, "How do you become president?" The entire table froze and looked at me like I was crazy. No one asks to be president; that is usually not done. Most of the time you have to be asked, then there's a process where the club must accept and vote you in. I was thrilled to be voted in. I will never forget what Miss Ann said to me.

Being the Queen of Rotary, she always knows what to say. As she put it so clearly, "It is simple, DiAnna, just think of how you want to change the world."

What? I can do that!

I will never forget those words, as I had the most incredible following year.

At my first meeting I remember saying, "I am DiAnna, your president for this year. One of my goals is to raise the bar and lower the podium."

I did accomplish that! Two things I certainly learned from the beginning of my term—my passions are not everyone's passions and my standards are not everyone's standards. If I was going to make a difference I had to lead by example. Boy, have I grown since my first class when I developed T.A.S.K.

When leading a community service event, instead of saying, "How many of you are coming?" I would say, "Who would like to join me in some fun?"

That simple little phrase got a lot of work done!

My greatest accomplishment that year was receiving a global grant that helped us build a music academy in Jinotepe, Nicaragua. One hundred dollars from the Jinotepe Rotary Club, joined with $5,000 from an anonymous angel in our club, was all sent to Rotary International Foundation. That is where the magic of Rotary took place, as the foundation soon sent us a check for $19,000 which changed the world in Jinotepe, Nicaragua.

It took two years to complete the academy with Instruments and instructors, students and facility. It was like a community of joy all came together.

The fire station housed the instruments and made room for a classroom and the university provided the instructors. It was a team of joy and an honor to be part of something so much bigger than me!

Not too long after completion, we all celebrated with two of my cherubs bringing their own mouthpieces from home as they played together with the local students when the city celebrated us. They played the American and the Nicaraguan national anthems together, with the locals on the instruments we had made possible.

That became one of the greatest accomplishments I felt in that year; however every little bit made a big difference and we did a lot!

I do believe no task is too tiny to make a big difference, no pun intended, and talk about a million smiles!

A smile is just a smile until you give it away! Nothing so simple, nothing as sweet, as the universal language of a smile. It is priceless.

Photo with Gary C.K. Huang,
Rotary International President 2014-'15

— — — — — — — — • • •

What I give is what I get in those special moments with a simple smile on my cheek. I don't expect it back, yet it wins every time. How can you not smile back when someone gives you their time?

You never know who is looking and you never know what a smile will do. When you simply give a part of you.

A smile is a smile as it will take you miles away from your plan just by raising your hand!

♫♪

"Can't Stop The Feeling"
Justin Timberlake

"

*You will never follow your own
inner voice until you clear up
the doubts in your mind.*

"

Roy T, Bennett

CHAPTER 18

THE RAT, THE CAT AND THE GECKO

Value: Listening

Think of what scares you the most! A spider, a clown, or even a sweet little lady bug. Whatever your greatest fear is, multiply that fear by 100 and that is how scared I am of a sweet little rat and a gecko, too.

Forget it! I am out of there!

When we are quiet we really can hear a lot, some in our minds, some in our surroundings, mostly in our intuition. When we allow ourselves to be quiet in all three, we can hear far more than whatever is actually there.

When going on a journey into the unknown in a country in despair, such as I did in Nicaragua, you must listen to that little voice that will guide you, warn you, and bring you home safely.

For me, the connections made and relationships built between the two countries have been nothing short of a blessing, both to myself and to all those I bring along on for a "cultural experience."

This particular trip developed my intuition so much more than I was ready for.

I had my team and my plan, my passport and budget, my bug repellant and my sleeping net. All I needed now was confirmation of no delays with our flight. I was ready. Or was I?

Since Frank had moved to Texas, now it is John Mims, Janet and me. We all had made this trip several times. We were ready! Ready to perform a dance of life with no words needed. We knew our parts and supported each other.

Now it was time to start having some fun, until I got that call and a man's voice that said, "I won't be going."

What?

Every fear I had of being alone crept right back up on my shoulder! Yes, Janet was going with me, but I still needed that man! For the first time in a long time, I felt very small.

> ...you are the pilot. now you just have to fly.
>
> – John Mims

Unforeseen reasons required John Mims to stay home. He told me with confidence, "You got this. You are ready."

I quickly replied with no breath in my lungs, "I don't think that is true. I cannot do this without you!"

He said all so calmly, "Oh yes you can, you are the pilot, now you just have to fly. You have been preparing for this!"

I then said "The trip, yes. Going without you, not so much!"
I continued, "What would I do if…"

To all of my "what ifs," he kept saying, "You got this."

How did he have so much confidence in me? All I could do was
panic, not knowing what to do?

Without his great patience, where would I be? He is John Mims
and I am just me! His patience and calming demeanor is a blessing.
Without John Mims where would I be?

Of course I knew I had to go. I had a team depending on me, yet
my breath and my heart was saying, "Not just yet!" That's when
I had to look back in time and know that I could do this even
without John Mims. At this point I had no choice. I had a team of
twelve all packed and ready to go.

I believe he knows by now how much he is appreciated for all that
he has done to rescue my spirit with his gentle guided plans. I say
that meaning, he always has my back! Rarely saying a word, just
quietly in the background taking pictures and holding the space for
the cherubs, Janet and me too, allowing us to explore and grow in
every step taken though this life-changing door.

A trip like this is no vacation; it is so much more. The cherubs have
been known to call him "Papa John"—I knew he would be missed by
more than just me. I took him on my shoulder knowing if I were in
need, I would simply say to myself, "What would John Mims do?"

Before we left, he said, "Go with your intuition and you will know what to do!" I knew this was true, yet I still felt that fear. I had come to rely on some things, like knowing John Mims would not laugh at me or judge me or even whisper, "It's just a bug." He would catch that bug if he knew it would help Janet and I sleep better at night.

Did I mention Nicaragua has lots of bugs?

Our flight was scheduled to leave in three days. Was that enough time for me to re-plan? Nothing major, just missing one man. Several boys were making the trip. It was important for them to have that MAN figure for any "boy issues" at hand, some only a "dad" could handle.

I had another dad going with us, yet it wasn't the same. I knew this father was not prepared to take on a leadership role.

Off we went with one thousand pounds of donations and so much more. The greatest gift was being a team with open arms.

One lesson I have learned in all my Rotary training for international projects, is that you must build a trusting relationship with your chosen country. You must set your course so they know you are authentic. So many people show up with cameras, paint brushes and treats, then disappear after a week.

It is those who return and keep their word who receive that respect, a bond, and a dear friendships too.

Having that friendship and that bond with Casa de Angel, a hostel so sweet, meant they would have "my bedroom" ready. This was our fifth year in Nicaragua, so I felt very comfortable with no despair.

We entered our room so nice and clean. I thought for sure I would sleep like a queen. Janet and I had set up our room ready for the troops. All we needed to do was prepare for the next day. Tonight we thought we would just let the cherubs sleep because we knew what was coming.

Or did we?

Lying quietly in my bed, my head was spinning. Then I heard the sound of little feet. No, not the cherubs, but from a rat we had named Ricky. Now remember, my fear is 100 times greater than whatever you fear. Yep, it was a rat!

This little guy was right above my head, somewhere above the very low plywood ceiling. Too close for comfort! Only a thin layer of plywood separated me from that rat! I could hear him nibble; I could hear him shuffle. I was ready for him to find a new home. Not my luck!

No more thought of sleeping like a queen. I just became the guardian of the gate. I prayed I would sleep just a wink. Exhausted from the flight, I knew I had to rest. Would I be any good if I was put to a test, or over exhausted because of a rat? I didn't have John Mims with me, and I kept hearing him say, "You got this."

Little did I know Ms. Janet had a friend, too! She had the cat that pounced above her in that same low ceiling above her head. Did these little critters know we were coming, and were they planning to scare us on purpose? Did they know this was "our room" and that we did not want to share?

For three days I tried not to listen to those two little creatures of God pounce. They certainly did not play. On the night before we left, Janet and I both heard a big MEOW. Needless to say, "bye-bye baby," no more rat! None too soon, as we were leaving the hostel that day by noon.

Next we traveled to Granada, where we had magical moments and completed several projects in five cities in six days. I was ready for a good night's rest. The cherubs were incredible and all our projects were priceless experiences with everything and more than we ever expected. Denis was an angel and worth his weight in gold. We could not have managed this trip without our "local friend" who has worked his way into our hearts.

He started out as our translator and quickly became our local team coordinator. He made so much more magic happen than I could have ever planned. This is a man who taught himself English by listening to the Beatles and singing "Imagine." A man of music and of my own heart.

I keep telling him, "You are a male me," meaning his demeanor, his playful ways, his magnetic guidance with the cherubs, and his love for music is certainly a shadow of me. I say this with sincere respect and great humor too. I have found a second me.

I found another me in a man named Denis. Over time, we've danced our teamwork, sometimes without saying any words. We just know what to do, him in English and me in hysterical Spanish. Over there, he is my shadow.

He not only translates my words but also my emotions and my heart too. That makes him worth so much more than his weight in gold!

With very few words, a single phrase "Johnny Walker" is my cue to not do something, such as speaking English in a crowd that does not smile in a friendly manner to tiny redhead Americans. For sure they would know I was not a local. Ya' think?

With my curly, red hair and freckles too, plus snow white skin, all I would have to do is just open my mouth and the locals would know I was not one of them. However, when they noticed my blue eyes, they would always wink. I don't think they thought for one moment I belonged, yet I felt they knew I wasn't a threat.

Making our way through the streets of Granada we returned to the Chocolate Mansion. No, it was not a chocolate factory; it was a beautiful spa hotel in the center of town, surrounded by breathtaking views that included a historical church and many children too in the streets looking for food and something to drink.

In the plaza of Granada, Nicaragua
Se llama Inmaculada Concepcion de Maria,
aka Cathedra de Granada

. . .

The sights that we saw were overwhelming to say the least and since we had left the hostel, I felt it would be a good treat for the cherubs to spend one night at a hotel with a pool and different showers. Although our sweet little hostel had showers and good plumbing, there was something to be said about a place with no rat.

We arrived at the hotel with great joy after spending time in the central plaza with tons of tourists and vendors too. All I kept hearing was, "Cuanto dinero por favor?" (How much money please?)

Now it was late and time to register for our rooms. Much to my dismay, they had put me and Janet at one end of the hotel with the cherubs and the dad on two different floors. Talk about trust and believing all would be well!

Once again, I was so tired I could hardly tell you my name. I pulled a quick meeting and told the cherubs all NOT to leave the hotel no matter what, no matter how much music they heard in the streets! Did I believe they would all stay in? What would you think since two of them were 18? Guess what the "legal age" in Nicaragua is? Some may have thought, "What she doesn't know, she cannot tell my momma."

My intuition said I knew better than that! Of course, one or more would see what they could discover. I did make it clear, "If you make a poor choice, your momma will have to come get you at her expense and I know you would not make her make that choice!"

Now that the cherubs were settled in, I was off to my room guided by starlight and a bright shining moon. Little did I know what Nicaragua's star lights bring … You guessed it, a new little friend!

Janet was standing in our room with her face toward the main wall. I looked at her and saw her eyebrow raise! Holy cow, what could it be that would cause such a look? It certainly frightened me! She calmly said, "Don't turn your head." All I could think was, "What the crud, not again!"

With her still looking up at the wall I knew I had to suck it up and see what it was that had grabbed her attention. As I turned my head, all I could see was this wiggly tail going into a hole, high on the wall. "Oh hell no, not again. I will not share my room with another little friend!"

Janet looked at me and laughed. She knew how frightened I was and said, "What are we going to do about this?"

Well, I marched myself, more like ran, right to the registration desk to find a man. I tried to explain, "There is a critter in my wall and is going in and out with a long tail. Can you get a ladder and come get it out?

Where was John Mims???

The man at the desk looked at me and smiled. Then I heard him say with laughter in his voice, "It's only a gecko and they live here too!" He thought I was funny, yet little did he know how frightened I was to the point of having no words!

As I was walking away, the dad who was with us said, "What has you so upset?" I explained about the gecko and he quickly said in a stern voice, "Suck it up, it's just a gecko."

I knew right then he was no replacement for our dear John Mims with a great big heart, who always makes the situation better and would never say such words.

Did I sleep? Oh, yes I did, in my peppermint-scented net which I knew that bad boy gecko could not get through! One thing I knew was my extra little friends, the rat, the cat and the gecko, were not going to stop me from having any magical moments this "cultural experience" had planned for me. They were part of the culture and my experience was maybe they were providing a lesson to get over some fears.

By the way, for all those who are curious, each and every cherub was at breakfast the next day without any notices from the local police!

♫♪

"The Best Day of my Life"
American Authors

"

What happens when people open their hearts?
They get better.

"

Haruki Murakami

CHAPTER 19

IF ONLY

Value: Vulnerability

So many times in the area of love, I felt like I was being tested, like I was on the edge of failure or loss. I believe that if love is a test, there should be a pop quiz at the end of every day to confirm we both are still connected and living the real fairytale that is meant to be.

They say, "third time's the charm." Is it? I am still asking that question.

I am an old-fashioned Southern girl who believes in love.

Does the fairy tale really exist?

I believe it does, because you make your own fairy tale.

In the movie Maleficent, Maleficent thought she put that dreadful sleep curse on Aurora and "only the kiss of true love" would wake her. Little did she know it was her own kiss that broke the curse, not the prince!

A wise woman once told me, "You can't help who you love." Maleficent did not know she loved Aurora as she did and it was only when she opened her heart, asked for forgiveness and kissed her with true love that Aurora woke up!

I thought I was in love; I believe I was. He was nine when he told me he was going to marry me in ten years and that is what happened. A childhood love met me at the altar as we said "I do." I was 20, he was 19. Married for 24 years and one day! Yep, he wanted to "honor" 24 years! We had a steak dinner one night and signed divorce papers the next day

I had grown up, gotten stronger and discovered we wanted different things in life. Our paths were definitely going in different directions and I woke up to the fact that I cannot clap with one hand. It takes two hands to put sound into the purpose of the clap and it takes two to make a marriage magical.

If I sat with myself of 14 years ago, I would look at that version of myself and say, "Don't worry, you will be happy. You will see."

She would say to me, "You are crazy, how will that be?"

I would say, "Wait and see, just believe, trust, breathe, and keep taking one step at a time. It will all be okay." If only I knew then what I know now!

I took her advice. As a Life Coach, I have learned how to be my own best coach. At the end of the day I know it is "me, myself, and I" and I never let me down. I love me for me and I will always be here for me. I know life is short and Lord knows I am short enough! Did I say I am 4'8" tall with shoes on?

I keep saying, I am not vertically challenged, I am energetically tall! That energy took me right into my next, I thought, Prince

Charming's arms. He was 20 years my junior yet the same age of my soul. He was actually my "partner-in-joy" who was part of my whirlwind life during Hurricane Katrina. How can you feel you have finally found your soulmate, only life has a different plan? Talk about a fairy tale.

"You cougar you." That's what everyone would say. I believe this man would have painted my toenails on my deathbed. He never had any judgments when it came to my looks, my body size, or conversations that took us into the wee hours of the night.

> " I'm not vertically challenged, I am energetically tall! "

So what happened? A curse of some sort found its way in. Did I eat a bad apple? Who knows? I do know trust and communication is the key to all success. With age comes maturity and different choices. Enough said.

Then there were three! They say, "third time's the charm." Is it?

He walked up to my desk at work and asked, "Are you married yet?"

I said, "Nope, my Prince Charming hasn't shown up yet."

He quickly replied, "He just did."

What?!? OH MY WORDS, my heart stopped! I had had a crush on this man back in the day... We had flirted for years as we passed each other in town after we both divorced. Oh ... my ... words, did

I die and go to heaven? Is it true? Did my Prince Charming really show up?

I am a Chatty-Cathy, but at that moment I was without words. I smiled big and thought, "Really?"

We texted for a couple weeks and when I said, "I don't share my milk or my men," he said in his humorous way, "Got milk?" I ran!

We did not speak for a few months after that.

At that point I did not know if I was really ready for a relationship after the last one, whom I'd thought was my soulmate, made a different choice.

Then, one day I was leaving work with a real serious face, not my normal smiling one.

Without my seeing him, my Prince Charming drove by and texted me later. He asked if I was okay and that's all it took. We met for coffee on New Year's Eve and enjoyed each other's laughter. I am talking giggles from the belly laughter.

After a few weeks of enjoying time together, I ask him, "So why did you text me again after I ran?"

He said, "I don't know. When I drove by and you weren't smiling, I thought you needed a friend."

I looked at him and smiled even bigger. I said, "I have never caught a man's attention because I wasn't smiling."

He makes me laugh from my belly, calms my soul like no other and he is always happy. You ask him, "How was your day?" and he always says, "It is always good." He is what every woman wishes for. An easy-going, happy man. Who wouldn't want that? I want that. I deserve that.

They say be careful what you ask for. I remember saying, "I have many friends to do things with, but I want that one special someone to do nothing with."

Winnie the Pooh says it so preciously, "When you do nothing, it leads you to the very best something".

I got what I asked for. Yep, I love spending quiet time and doing nothing but being together in the moment. However, I do realize sharing more of our lives together is really what I would like because I love so much about him.

His thought: "Take it slow, go with the flow."

The first time I said "I love you," I felt like Maleficent put a spell on him. She put that "unbreakable wall" spell on him and I don't know if "true love's kiss" can break that spell. Not knowing his past, only knowing what joy there is between us, makes me definitely practice patience. I keep being the silly, affectionate me ... and he keeps calling me. Does he know why? Nope, nor do I. Yet I am glad he does because one thing I know, he calms my soul like no other. Will that wall ever come down; will this "friendship" ever change? Only time will tell.

For me, when someone is very important and special in my life, I tell them I love them. I let them know how important they are to me and I make time for that relationship.

Girl time is great, mommy time is incredible, friends are what put the "wine of life" in the glass of joy, and don't even speak to me about "grammie time." If there is anything wrong in my world, I just put myself in the presence of the grandchildren. I have eight. When times are tough, nothing else in the world matters at that moment except Colton, Makenzie and Ryder too, Audrey and Peyton, Eden, Riley and Jacqueline to boot. Who could be sad in the presence of such joy in the world? That's what really matters. I am living the dream. My heaven is on earth.

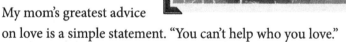

There are many meanings of love and I believe we are put on this earth to love and to be loved.

My mom's greatest advice on love is a simple statement. "You can't help who you love."

That statement makes me think of what love is, what it feels like, the love I have had in my life and the love I want in my life.

I have learned that if you keep your heart open, even when it hurts, it will be filled with the love that was meant to be and was put here on earth for you and me. It will be the fairy tale if we allow it to birth.

My Prince Charming turned out to be "the king." I ask myself, does he want a queen in his kingdom? Nope, not right now. If that doesn't throw the fairy tale to the wind, I don't know what will.

We are great "friends" and I treasure our time together. My tummy tingles just seeing his smile and my soul screams "Yahoo!" when he says, "What's up with you?"

With each relationship I learned defined lessons. The first, marriage is great if all hands are clapping together. If you treasure each other, nothing else matters.

In the second, age is just a number. It doesn't matter what others think. Go with your heart, trust and be honest, communicate, and the rest will follow.

The third lesson is never hold your words back. Something might be said that will change your world forever.

A major lesson I have learned in life and love is to allow yourself to be vulnerable when you find yourself discovering "the one." I have discovered it is not about your childhood love or your soul mate or even your Prince Charming.

I believe it is about "the one," the one who is meant and waiting for you and you for him.

It is "the one" that completes your puzzle of life. I do believe to get to this place, being vulnerable is the magical piece of that puzzle. Allowing yourself to drop all the walls of defense and accept the love that is so graciously waiting for you. And talk!

Talk, talk, and talk some more! Let yourself be known. At least your dos and don'ts … What you will accept and what is a deal breaker. We don't always know what we want, yet we certainly know what we don't want!

When in an adult relationship and both are open to each other, the greatest conversations are in your birthday suit. Yep, because you are most vulnerable in the suit you were brought into this world with. When you are living in the moment and loving the skin you are in, believe me, your communication goes to a different realm and there is less chance of one or the other stomping out of the room. Sometimes there are no words. Quiet time and body language says it all. I am not talking sexual conversations or gestures … I am speaking of the connection and the joy that can be discovered in allowing yourself to be so vulnerable.

If you have ever seen the movie Pretty Woman, you must remember the bathtub scene where Edward (Richard Gere) is sitting in front of Vivian (Julia Roberts), and her legs are wrapped around him. She says, "Did I mention my leg is 44 inches from hip to toe, so basically we're talking about 88 inches of therapy wrapped around you for the bargain price of …"

It is true, "water talks" can wash the tough parts of life away and those are priceless moments. Not holding back what is really in your heart and putting it into words could be that magical puzzle piece that completes you.

It is not always about making love physically, it is about connecting to the core. Communication is not always about the physical word, it is about hearing the words that are not being spoken.

Am I "with" someone at the moment you ask? Life will tell!

Do I go online? Do I close my heart to love? Do I just go with the flow?

A six-foot-tall man once said to me, "You intimidate me."

I looked at him and said, "What is it about this four-foot, eight-inch woman that intimidates you?"

> " It's not your size, it is your energy. It is so much bigger than your body. When you walk into a room, you don't have to say anything, you just are.
>
> – Six-foot-tall Man "

He said, "It's not your size, it is your energy. It is so much bigger than your body. When you walk into a room, you don't have to say anything, you just are."

I did not know what to do with that statement at that moment. At this moment, I would say take it and shine.

Shine, baby, shine! Don't hold back an ounce of that beautiful energy! I would not have said that so many years ago, yet now is my magical moment and I do believe we all deserve to shine, each and every one.

Does that energy give me the courage to walk into a new relationship? It would if I allowed it and trusted the process of the universe. It would if that is what I wanted.

In today's world there is every type of "dating" possibility. Websites, speed dating, blind dates. It all starts with signing up, one contract or another. You name it, they have it! Yet I often think, what happened to the good ol' fashioned, simple boy meets girl, girl smiles and the rest is history?

Does that still exist? Is that the fairy tale?

So many directions, so many menus to choose from. So many pictures to pick from. Swipe this way or that.

I think I want to be the woman with all the cats! NOT!

I know you have heard that proverbial saying from Alfred Lord Tennyson, "It is better to have loved and lost than to never have loved at all."

Forrest Gump put it so simply and so profoundly when he said to his Jenny, "I may be a stupid man, but I do know what love is."

There are so many levels and degrees of love! I love you like this ... I will love you if ... I love you just because! It is all so simple, right and wrong!

Love is a great challenge, yet the greatest reward.

I love this quote from Norwegian writer Arne Garborg, "To love a person is to learn the song that is in their heart and to sing it to them when they have forgotten."

I am so grateful for truly knowing love, including all the pain and tears that are a part of it. Yes, pain and tears are a part of loving. It is only then that the sleeping beauty (YOU) really wakes up to "true love."

For me, no prenuptials are needed. No long, many-page contract. Just a sweet little four line statement:

> *Court me.*
> *Love me.*
> *Make me happy.*
> *Seal it with a kiss.*

Pretty simple, right? Wrong again! For some, it is not that simple. However, life can be pretty simple if you let it be. You don't give up on the one you love. You still love them and thank them for the gifts they share with you and the lessons learned for this season in your life.

I have discovered through this journey to today, the beauty and love within. The LIGHT that shines, the JOY that bubbles and the PEACE that weaves my entire life together.

When I feel I am fighting love battles I will never win or feel as if I am swimming upstream against all odds and truly think I will not see the sunlight of love in my world, I always find my strength by going to my heart and listening to my body.

In silence you can hear a lot from your heart, mind, and soul. They will never let you down. I go to my tummy in particular and listen to what it says. Yep, it says more than just hunger. I always ask myself those tough questions and if my heart is at peace and my tummy has butterflies of joy, I know my decision is right. If my heart is racing and my tummy is anxious, well then, I hold my hands up high and ask for guidance!

I do believe, never ask a question unless you are ready to hear the answer. When you are ready, everything else will fall into place.

Sometimes when we get to know someone, we get to know ourselves even more.

I have experienced so many people who will say, "If only he loved me, I would be complete," or, "If only he ... I would be ..."

I did that too! I thought a man would complete my puzzle of life.

What I have discovered is that I do not need a man to complete my life, I want a man in my life. I complete ME.

A man in my life to share that puzzle would complete my life as a joyous bundle.

Paula Noble Fellingham, one of my mentors, once said, "Love is what we aspire to; the connection is what completes us."

Having that one special person, the one you can say, "You are my person," for some that is the puzzle piece that completes them. "The one" could be the last frog you kiss that turns into your prince. And the fairy tale begins!

I feel so much love in my life and I am so in love with life.

Together, me and my sweet little Southern inner child Sissy, who always loves me has embraced a pretty challenging life and a joyful learning journey!

YOU CAN TOO!

Here is my formula, my four favorite "F" words: Faith, Family, Friends, and Fun. With those four fabulous favorites, life always has your back. I invite you to take the ride with your hands up as if you are on a scary-but-fun rollercoaster ride. That is the ride we call life. YAHOO! It really is all so yummy!

♩♫♪

"A Million Dreams"
Ziv Zaifman

"

If you want to go fast, go alone.
If you want to go far, go together.

"

Henderson & Bias Robinson

CHAPTER 20

OOPS, I FORGOT TO STOP

Value: Play

"Play, passion and purpose, all leads to progress." That is what I said while looking out the window to a vision I had doodled on paper for years. What I found in Utah started back in Mississippi when I was a small child.

As an adult young at heart, everything I teach, I teach through interactive play. In my mind, who doesn't want to play? Who doesn't want to have fun? Who doesn't want to let that little one, you, discover that fun in the sun? Who doesn't…? As it turns out, too many to count.

I have learned over the years that many people are afraid to show who they are and allow that little one inside themselves to play.

I have been accused many times of "living in a fantasy world" yet I am here to tell you my world is real. It is alive and it is very colorful.

I saw this beautiful poster; it reminds me of my fantasy world …

My unicorn carries me when I am weak; my colors delight me when I am blind. And the stars are waiting for me to reach. My world is real and my colors sparkle. That is how I choose to live my life.

In a city park in San Marcos, Nicaragua, I forgot to stop at the bottom of a slide. Yep, I fell right on my back and scared the crude out of all the cherubs and Denis too. He was filming everyone going down the slide and in all my playfulness I thought, "Why not me? I am not too old to go down that slide too."

I loved the slide and I climbed right up the ladder of brightly painted tires to get to the top. I remember feeling so exuberant from the work we had just completed. In that moment at the top of the slide I felt like I could fly like a bird! So off I went, down that slide, my arms wide open to the world. It was dark outside and the stars lit up the sky. I remember looking up in amazement and feeling like I was invincible in the moment.

The length of time it took to get down that slide was how long it took me to realize just how invincible I was NOT! Bam! I hit the ground. That sure woke me up from my "delusional" being. Everyone jumped to my rescue and all I could do was laugh and say, "I am okay. Really, I am okay." I knew everyone instantly must have thought, "This old woman just broke a hip." Nope, not me.

All I could do at that moment was laugh. One, for being totally embarrassed, secondly, for being so grateful that I did not break a hip, and finally, because I had had so much fun in that moment.

All I could think and say was, "Oops, I forgot to stop."

Those words took me far beyond my imagination. It confirmed to me that we should never stop playing, no matter our age. No matter our challenges, no matter what people say. I plan to always play.

I give a million heart-filled thanks to a country in such despair for the beauty and love they continue to share. For the soul connections that will never end. For the friendships that will forever stand and for being there at the end of that slide!

While still doing and planning for what is next in my "second home," Nicaragua, I found myself going to Utah. Utah you say? Why there when you have so much more to do in Nicaragua?

Well, let me tell you. Finding my purpose, finding my connection to me, and finding my moment when I knew I am on the right path— that is what took me to Utah. My path and my purpose showed up again in Utah.

Being invited into a handpicked group of phenomenal women, into a group called Circle of Women, led by Paula Noble Fellingham, confirmed I was on my way to "my volcano exploding with SKITTLES" and I dared not stop.

Let me briefly mention how I met Paula.

While at the 100 year celebration of Rotary Foundation at the International Conference in Atlanta, Georgia, Paula was a keynote speaker for the Peace Conference two days prior. She used words from my vocabulary in her presentation like "fun and yummy, love and peace." Listening to her presentation, I thought, "I must get to this woman." With several thousand people in the room I could not get close to her, yet I was able to get her literature with the plan of emailing her when I returned home.

She was for sure a woman of my own heart and I wanted to meet her.

Two days later, guess what happened? We both were in the same room, same time, and crossed paths. I saw her coming, not sure if it was her. As she got closer, I could see her light up with a smile as I smiled back. She looked at me and said, "Your smile is so sweet." Being humbled with that, I replied, "Well, thank you. If happiness is sweet, that is me."

I chuckled and she grabbed my shoulders, turned me to face her eye-to-eye and said, "No, you have a glow. I want to know you!" What? A woman of her great caliber wanted to know me! What do you do with that when someone with her confidence, her enthusiasm, and her brilliance, says that to you?

You say, "Okay." That's what I did.

Still not knowing for certain who she was, we spoke for about three minutes then I said, "Were you the keynote speaker at the Peace Conference!?"

She quickly replied, "Yes."

I knew the stars were aligned. She looked me in the eye and said, "You have a story. I want to know it—I want to work with you!" She continued, "I hand-pick strong women from around the world to work together for a year as they discover their ultimate excellence. I want to work with you."

Was this real? Was she real? What do I have that intrigued her to stop and talk to me?

There were 40 thousand Rotarians at this conference and she picked me.

Mind blowing. Very impressed. Very honored and still not sure.

Yet, I was game!

I returned home and we spoke one week later.

Here I am today accomplishing what she guided and encouraged me to do—find my voice, my confidence, my courage and my creativeness to put my story out there.

Little did she know I have had this book on a vision board on my wall, including the title, for over 14 years. I just did not have the confidence or the courage, nor did I make the time. At the time, I did not believe that anyone other than her would want to know my story.

Paula hand-picked, in person, 12 women from around the world, brought us together online and guided us to move closer to "Our Total Excellence." The one-year program in which she mentored us met once a week online. In addition, all 12 of us supported each other. After two months of meeting online, we all came together at a retreat in Utah where we worked with Paula as we encouraged, empowered and embraced each other's beauty and brilliance.

Again, I had to beat the gremlins off my shoulders. Who was I to get hand-picked? Who was I to be a part of this phenomenal circle of women? What did I have to bring to the circle? I quickly discovered—ME—all of the great me!

I would not have said that years ago. Yet through surmounting the adversities, developing my personal values and accepting all the opportunities, I discovered that if I do not walk through the doors that open, I will never see what is on the other side.

What I experienced and discovered through the window of a lake house in Saratoga Springs, Utah, opened my eyes to the fact that once again, I was in the right place at the right time. Doing just what I was meant to do. Talk about invigorating!

I arrived at the retreat a day early to make sure I would get settled in and be ready for the "work" I knew would begin the next morning.

Three of us arrived early. We were taken from Paula's home to the lake house where the wonderful work and the delight of discovering the excellence in us would be revealed.

It was a three-story, ten bedroom, seven bath home filled with family fun, full of life and love shared by many. I felt the energy of the home the moment I walked in.

We three girls were given a tour by the dear heart homeowner named Susan who shared her family home with us for a week.

She said, "Pick your room." Little did I know what was behind my door!

I picked my room because it was on the top floor; it was the only room with a window to the lake and it had a stencil painting on the wall that said, "Be strong and courageous." I did not need to look at any more rooms. I knew this one was for me.

The next day, I woke up to a beautiful sunrise outside my window. I was enjoying the breathtaking surroundings, then I saw it.

I saw the exact simple scene I had been doodling for years! The exact shape of the mountains, the exact position of the sun between the mountains, the exact time of day, morning sunrise. Oh my words! That view took my breath away.

It told me, once again, I was in the right place at the right time. I knew I had to absorb all I could learn from this great opportunity I had received just because I had smiled at someone!

I knew this was a miracle in a moment I was born to see!

That moment made me reflect back to a story my mom told me after I'd grown up, one that bothered her dearly as it had happened to her in the dark.

With great concern, I asked her if she was okay telling me the story. She had mentioned it years before, yet never told me the whole story. She replied, "I believe you should know. I just don't know if it matters."

Sitting around the table, we all listened as she told the story.

"Your Aunt Doris and I were out one night in an alley. I can't remember why we were there and we had all six of you kids. The boys were already in the car and Aunt Doris and I were putting you and Tina in next.

"A very old woman came up to you and touched you on the shoulder. She looked at me and said, 'This baby is going to be a genius,' and then she walked away. She scared me so bad I grabbed you and looked at Aunt Doris and said, 'Did you see that?' and even faster she said, 'Yes! Let's get out of here!'

"I looked back and the old lady was gone. We were never so scared in our lives."

And that's all she said. She's never spoken of it since.

Now looking at the definition of genius, I never considered myself or call myself a genius.

I looked up the definition of genius by doing a google search. This is what I found:

1. *a person who is exceptionally intelligent or creative, either generally or in some particular respect.*

Reading that made me blush. But I pushed myself to read on, not allowing a single gremlin to find its way into my space.

2. *a person regarded as exerting a powerful influence over another for good or evil.*
3. *the prevalent character or spirit of something such as a nation or age.*

As I looked at the definition of what that word really means, and knowing it was a story about myself told of a moment in time … I would still never call myself a "genius." Yet, I accept that moment in time and embrace it all with grace. I would much rather say I am just DiAnna doing what I love rather than claim to be a genius. It certainly does not take a genius to know your values, acknowledge your adversities and discover your victories. I believe everyone has a "genius" within. Finding that part of you could be a big part of your own joyous journey.

I turned 60 years young on Election Day, November 6, 2018.

I voted for me to never stop living and never stop loving.

I voted for me to always see the light in every soul.

I voted for me to absolutely embrace being 60 and sensational because I choose to do so!

And I also did my citizen duty and voted at the pole.

I forgot to stop at the bottom of that slide in Nicaragua. I will not forget to stop doing what I do because I love it so!

The slide where "I forgot to stop" in the village park in San Marcos, Nicaragua

I do what I love and was born to do. Live, love life and open the door for others!

🎵🎶🎵

"Happy"
Pharrell Williams

66

A positive change, a positive domino effect.

99

Kelly Clarkson, Musician

CHAPTER 21

AWAKE

Value: Love

My journey is ongoing and it will not stop till the good Lord
chooses me to join the angels and dance in heaven with Elvis,
Michael Jackson, Lindsey, my brother Joe, too, and so many
more friends and loved ones I adore. Yet till that day, I am sure
to do the dance of life as life sings me a happy tune.

Along with the whole world, I heard a different song on the day
our world started dancing to a different tune.

One Friday, March 13, 2020, my world changed, again! Not just my
world but the entire world. That was the day our school campus,
and my job too, closed down as we went into "shelter in place."
We were told to do everything from home. That was the day
COVID-19 hit so close to home. We all are now fighting a silent
war. Not a war with guns, nor tanks, nor deployments, a silent
war on humanity that has taken thousands of lives. This war is not
picky on who it takes down: not by race, not by financial status,
and certainly not by age. This war is not prejudiced. Black, brown,
yellow, or white, it has taken many with no delight.

Our front liners are doctors, nurses, custodians, morgue directors, medics, police, and firefighters, too. Our essential workers include grocery store staff, bankers, and farm workers as well. Even my son, the Coca-Cola manager, goes to work on the battleground so we can stay home safe in our rooms. They wear the gloves and masks of survival for this war as it continues to take more. So we fight together to save more!

We pray for the safety of each man, woman, and baby as we watch the front lines change daily.

This war has affected not just one or two countries, it has affected our entire world. Many of us did not see it coming. The requirement to "shelter in place" put a whole new twist on a war like this.

Going into my bungalow alone and prepared opened my eyes to a whole different world.

I, for one, as accustomed in the past to live in my happy place, must constantly remind myself, "If I do not have control of the situation, I can most of the time stay positive and make light of the situation that is not right." For sure, this silent war has challenged me to the core of my soul and so much more. I believe as horrific as it is, it has woken us up to humanity and the call to heal not just this virus but our own brilliant selves.

What are the weapons and what is our ammunition? How can we fight something we cannot see? We can only believe. We can believe that it will get better, we can believe that it won't! Or we can stand together and unite as one. Our defense is our hearts, our compassion, too. Wear a mask and be sure to wash your hands to boot! One world, one heart, one fight. Something no other war has dared to master.

From the beginning of time, it has been proven history repeats itself in one way or another, if we are wise enough to view it and awake enough to see it. Rock 'n' roll never died and bell-bottom pants held strong fast to the fashion. With John Lennon glasses, everyone was cool. Yet with no vaccine in sight and Hazmat gowns the new fashion statement, a mask makes you look cool. How would we have known?

The Spanish flu, the Great Depression, and World War II. Who would have known we'd be right back there today without warning.

I recall learning in history class what President Franklin D. Roosevelt said right before so many men were drafted or enlisted to fight World War II: "Every man, woman, and child is in action."

He continued, "There is a mysterious cycle in human events. To some generations, much is given. Of other generations, much is expected. This generation of Americans has a rendezvous with destiny."

He was right, yet who would have known we would be there again with a different fight?   Rosie the Riveter said it just right, "We Can Do It!" and "Together We'll Win!"

75 years later and with much more wisdom, Harry Smith, a great historian, said of wars, "All of American's hearts beat as one." Let's take this wisdom and fight as one.

I love history and once heard a veteran and member of "the greatest generation" speak of World War II. Ed Kolinski, with his genuine smile and his humbled heart, was asked what made him great. I heard him simply say, "Greatness is thrust upon you."

The difference between then and now is we must stand together.

We are being called to thrust ourselves into action to find our ammunition to conquer this adversity. Our fight is for humanity and a better today. No country, no county, no city is different or better. We are all fighting this battle until a cure is found. One of my many challenges in this battle is the lack of that human touch. No hugs or kisses. You must stand six feet apart from strangers, friends, and loved ones you don't want to harm, not knowing if you are a carrier of the virus. Knowing there was a cure on the horizon would make us cheer. It seems like only a test will let us know for sure if every single person can win this war.

Because of time and advanced knowledge, we are better equipped for this silent war we call COVID-19. In past wars against pandemics, we did not have the technology. I remember a time I even cursed at it. Not being tech-savvy, I often wanted to quit when I was presented with a new technological twist. I praise it now. Because of technology we are blessed to stay home safe and still fight the war.

As it was said of World War II, "Victory was in reach for a people with a common goal and a common purpose." I believe that saying should be on the shield of every warrior in our current world destiny.

This is history repeating itself, yet this time we are stronger and more aware as we stay home preparing for the battle against an invisible enemy that makes us all so scared.

More than 56 days in as I write this. Oh dear Lord, I pray, "Please don't let this exceed the Great Depression." There is currently no vaccine, nor a pill that has proven will allow us to walk away from COVID-19 as if it were the common cold. This is a silent war that we must unite behind as we reach that battle line to find a cure. This will require a victory in the Revolution of Values as we stand strong and not give in to fear, to be awake to what we all need. Patience, courtesy, and pure kindness, too, will win any war if we slow down and see the big picture.

It is not coincident that the well-known author known as SARK magically, colorfully and energetically showed up again. I have followed her for years. It is not coincidental that Coaches Training Institute (CTI) opened a Brilliant Conversation. It is not coincidental that I was watching TV at that moment they announced the Call To Unite, a 24-hour stream of phenomenal souls to encourage, inspire, and engage us all to stand as one, embrace our fears and fund the needy. This crisis has given the gift of time to many to find their strength in faith and family, as I believe Mother Earth is healing humanity. She has sent us to our homes and asked us to stay inside as we save the lives of others, to wash our hands and heal our hearts. She is asking us to think, to discover, to create, and to share, as we all are sent to our rooms and become aware. Going to my room has opened my eyes to the lessons I never knew were so deep in my soul. This is a war that has no limits; it has taken many men, women, and children. With tons of resources and support too, practicing your patience is a value of sorts.

In the time of quarantine, I was fighting my own battles deep in my head. I felt guilty thinking I wasn't doing enough as I was safe in my room. I was feeling the gloom. Seeing the pain all over the world, I felt helpless and did not know how to shed my tears of guilt and compassion. I was overwhelmed with appreciation for realizing how prepared and able I was to see. Being anxious a lot of the time, yet trying to stay positive, was a challenge of mine. Not realizing the full meaning, I have prayed for years, "Dear Lord, please help us to be prepared for this day you have given us." Once again I say, be careful what you ask for as He always has a plan and answers our prayers.

This day I am prepared for, yet not everyone is. So many are suffering, and so many have lost. I pray for their loved ones as I shed tears from my heart. Our hero is humankind and our great brilliant self as we unite as one to stand here and fight. Together we can defeat this silent war on humanity. We fight this battle with the power of one with no guarantee other than the sun will come up tomorrow.

I am more awake now than I ever imagined to the call from Mother Earth as we all heal humanity.

I have used this time to begin training to discover that part of me I have yet to learn. Solitude is one's own mind. As long as you are awake, you will find your greatest gifts. The world is waiting for you and your gifts. During this time, journaling saved my sanity. Documenting exercise, food intake and highlights of the day with photos of my walks and fun visits "at a distance" filled my heart with joy and appreciation for what I do have control of.

Funny how the universe works. Before the pandemic broke out, I received a notice from my Life Coaching training facility about a new vision for coaches. Desiring a "boost" in my training, I was preparing to register. Little did I know what the universe had in mind for my training! During this time of uncertainty, I was blessed to train not in person, yet in the virtual world. This allowed me to train globally, which opened my heart, my mind, and my soul too much deeper learning than I'd ever thought possible. These were lessons I knew I had to learn.

Never before in history, was every student in the world, including me, sent home to learn. Parents took on a whole other role as teachers and parents all wrapped up in one. Education has changed, that is for sure. Will I ever see the day again when I can give that compassionate hug without worry? I sure hope this passes soon as the human touch is our greatest immunity in a world under such sorts of challenges.

During the quarantine, through weekly virtual coaches' training meetings with CTI I felt as if I traveled around the world and trained with incredible like-minded souls.

Our world as we know it has changed and this training gave me tools to bring out a better me to be of better service to others. This change in our world does not have to be negative. To embrace it and accept it just makes it different. It gives us all an opportunity to choose how we make our way in this greater new world.

Sam House, the co-founder of Coaches Training Institute, guided us through some great conversations. After a powerful one, he simply said, "Being reminded of the paradox of life—that we are creating it as much as it is creating us—makes us more aware of the impact this virus is having in our world."

We ask ourselves, what is normal? I believe normal is what works best for oneself. Our world has changed, as it has in the past. What works for some does not work for others. I do hope this new way of life, this new normal, continues to celebrate everyone, at all levels of humanity, as it has battled for and celebrated during this time. This is a historical journey.

I ask you in all the adversity, what impacted you? What did you discover about you? How has this time in our world helped you recognize and prioritize your values and move forward to your victories? The love that has grown during this time of need is greater than ever and will win any war. Our brilliant minds and researchers too, doctors and nurses and essential workers, all are the strongest defense to call. We all stand strong on the front line of life as we are safe in our rooms, growing stronger each night.

These simple questions can open a door for you to embrace and move forward for more, a better YOU in your journey through this beautiful thing we call life. Become awake and help Mother Earth beat this silent war and heal ourselves for a happier, healthier better today.

♪♫♪

"Imagine"
John Lennon

"

It always seems impossible until it is done.

"

Nelson Mandela

CHAPTER 22

THROUGH THE YEARS

Value: Peace

For many years I found myself running to something. I just wasn't sure what it was. Years later I found myself actually training for a half marathon.

Never having been a "runner," I prepared for the run by putting together a "playlist" of my life for my iPod. I started with the day I was born. What song was number one? Then with each year through the years before my memory kicked in, I picked a yearly song based on what my uncle Allen always listened to. Then I started picking the song for each year which made me feel stronger, made me remember I could take another step. By the time I was done I had put together 56 songs. Yes, one song for each year and I was 54 years young when I "ran like a diva," pink tutu and all!

What a powerful tool. What a joyful project and what a wonderful way to get me to that finish line.

Just when I didn't think I could take one more step, that song came on that gave me strength that kept me going. Not being a runner, I amazed myself completing that marathon 14 minutes after my goal time.

Through this activity I discovered I could have been "running from my life." Instead, I was "running TO my life."

For me, that half marathon was a huge accomplishment and I enjoyed the tunes along the way. What I realized is, life is like a marathon. We don't even know we are running the race until we reach the finish line.

Music and marathons of life have been monumental moments most of my life.

You may have noticed at the end of each chapter there is a song noted. That song spoke to me at that period of time in my life.

As I did, I invite you to make a "playlist" of your life. It will sell millions if only in payment of "SKITTLES" because it is a part of the great you.

I must say, Elvis helped me through the years to discover the great me! He is my American Idol. His music has lightened my heart through many tears of joy and challenges.

For someone who was so extraordinarily larger than life, and surrounded by millions most of his life, I hear he was very lonely. Yet he found in his heart the gift of giving. Not for recognition, yet just to be kind. It filled his heart where there was something missing.

I discovered he was a great humanitarian. A man of my own heart. I have had the opportunity to see him twice in my lifetime. What a gift. For my 16th birthday, my "fairy godmother" called and said, "If you had one wish, what would it be?"

I instantly said, "To see Elvis."

She quickly replied, "Wish granted."

Years later with "my two dads," I was blessed to share a special time with the two men who helped raise me. We enjoyed a road trip to Graceland.

In awe, I touched the door knob and walked through the door Elvis walked through. After reading a speech he wrote, I knew he was a man of my own heart. I was overwhelmed with emotions as I thought of how a man I never met played such a big part in my life and what it all meant to me.

As he once said, "I figure all any kid needs is hope and the feeling he or she belongs.

At the front door of Graceland

. . .

243

If I could do or say anything that would give some kid that feeling, I would believe I had contributed something to the world." If he only knew what hope he gave to me!

The step through that door put me on the track that Elvis confirmed was the right track. A track to serving others, a track to dancing to our own music and a track that leads others to discovering their own dance and music that lights up their life.

Through the years I have also stood at the doorstep and sat on the porch swing of a man who had a dream and paved the way for me and so many more. His famous words, "I have a dream" fills my life with purpose, patience and promise that I, too, with determination, drive and delight will fight for freedom, peace and fellowship.

As a child I saw racial separation. As an adult I see it too. The difference is now we walk hand-in-hand knowing it is a fight we can withstand.

Going to the home of Martin Luther King, sitting in the pew listening to his taped "Sermon on the Mountaintop," was moving. Walking the streets of his neighborhood and standing in the museum among a life-size interactive display of "The March," I put myself next to a Mississippi girl and posed for a picture as if I was in the march. Little did anyone there know what that moment meant to me! How I saw my life change, how I felt my world move, and how I will never silence my voice again.

Being in Atlanta when I embraced his daughter Bernice in a hug that would last forever at a Rotary convention, it confirmed to me I was on the right track.

From birth to now I live with the delightful knowledge that color is grand as we all walk hand-in-hand! Seeing many colors of people and different countries in my life, I have grown to accept the fact that I am on the right track.

It hasn't been easy and not always so much fun, yet I always "reach for moon and find happiness in the stars."

As I reflect through the years, I see myself as a truly happy, well-seasoned, accomplished woman.

Pinning Dr. Bernice A. King with our Club's Rotary pin. An embrace of gratitude that will last a lifetime!

From a bayou baby to an international traveler.

From a fragile little soul who could barely whisper my name out loud in a crowd to becoming energetically loud.

From wanting to only be a mommy in life to going above and beyond, becoming a professional mommy to many.

From discovering pure happiness in the dumps of Managua, Nicaragua, where I felt I had reached the depths of the earth, only to discover a place closest to heaven at the peak of a prayer rock at the highest point in Barcelona, Spain.

From being a cheerleader, to being a cheerleader coach, to now a coach of life.

From crying a river of tears to filling an ocean with tears of joy.

From feeling smaller than an ant to standing taller than Lady Liberty in a time of despair. New York and the events of 9/11 will be with me for years.

From receiving a vaccine for chickenpox to receiving a booster in life as I am part of a journey in history witnessing the war of COVID-19. Taking part in healing humanity.

From not having a voice, to discovering my voice and finding the courage to put my story out there. What I have discovered in writing this book is by finding my voice and putting it in words on the pages, I have committed to making a difference. The difference I was born to make, even if it is in only one single soul.

Not long ago, I was sharing with a friend how I have had this book in my heart and on my vision board for years. I continued by saying, "once I decided to start writing it, for whatever reason the words are just spewing out and they are so colorful."

It was at that moment I realized…

This is my volcano of SKITTLES. I have erupted

with true, colorful sweet-tasting happiness and gratitude for life and all the love in it.

Though the years may mount up, I do not see myself aging. I see myself as seasoning and gracefully growing. Only with time comes wisdom, experience, and an overwhelming gratitude for this thing we call life!

I believe we do not have control over anyone or anything beyond ourselves. We do have control of how we see and react to the world around us.

Peace is not always perfect, yet it sure is priceless!

Peace to one and all as you find the joy in your journey.

♫♪

"The Impossible Dream"
Luther Vandross

ABOUT THE AUTHOR

When DiAnna is not spending time with family, which includes eight grandchildren, she is wearing her Rotary hat and often changes into her Life Coach hat. She also manages the attendance office at the local high school, working closely with the vice principal in charge of discipline. She claims to be the "nicest mean guy on campus," guiding all the "cherubs" in making better choices.

DiAnna believes she gets paid for "playing." She has found her "fountain of youth" working every day with students, parents, and the community. It has given her an open platform to bring her passion and purpose to the community and internationally through the nonprofit she founded and developed: T.A.S.K 4 U & Me Foundation, Inc., a 501(c)3 nonprofit. (Together Achieving Successful Kindness)

DiAnna continues to move forward as her community has recognized her passion. She was nominated for the "Salute to Small Business" award. But it is not the awards that keep her passion alive, it is the joy in the journey. Her heart and the power in the purpose inspire her to keep opening doors of opportunity both locally and internationally by taking students to Nicaragua for over nine years, teaching, learning, and having "a cultural experience." She is dedicated to bringing home the true gift of kindness, gratitude, and the deep meaning of togetherness to the local community.

Her studies in psychology, business, life coaching, light work, and leadership all have equipped her to reach further for possibilities never imagined, opening doors to dreams that are possible!

Made in the USA
Coppell, TX
25 August 2021

61176751R00138